SOSO ANTIQUITY CULTURE AND CIVILIZATION

WAKARA

MOHAMED BENTOURA BANGOURA

Edited by Dr. Kaemanje Thomas

Copyright © Mohamed Bentoura Bangoura.

All rights reserved. No part of this book may be reproduced in any form or by any electronic or mechanical means, including information storage and retrieval systems, without permission in writing from the publisher, except by reviewers, who may quote brief passages in a review.

Edited by Dr. Kaemanje Thomas

ISBN: 978-1-63732-548-3   (Paperback Edition)
ISBN: 978-1-63732-549-0   (Hardcover Edition)
ISBN: 978-1-63732-547-6   (E-book Edition)

Book Ordering Information

Phone Number: 315 288-7939 ext. 1000 or 347-901-4920
Email: info@globalsummithouse.com
Global Summit House
www.globalsummithouse.com

Printed in the United States of America

I would like to express my deepest thanks to the five dearests with whom I have had the good fortune to work: my brother Ibrahima Bangoura (accountant), Dr Ibrahima Deen Toure (pharmacist), Mr Ousmane Camara (former ambassador), Doctor Salifou Sylla (former rector of the University of Conakry Gamal Abdel Nasser), former Minister of Justice, Doctor Mohamed Rachid Toure (former President of the electoral system of Guinea and Sema instructors of the Sossoka tradition). My immense gratitude also goes to my mother, my father, my wife, Dr. Kaemanje Thomas, and of course to you my readers.

Never could I have written this book without the help and support of many people who gave their knowledge of the Soso culture generously. To all of you, thank you for your sincere contribution.

PREFACE

At the request of the coordination of the popularization of the kore-Sebeli alphabet and the charter of Kèmèkiriyah kayah, I have the honor to write the history of the Empire Soso. As far as Guinea is concerned, this task is not just an adventure but a major undertaking. First, let me express my gratitude to the President Abdoul Soumah and members of the Soso Coordination Office in the United States of America, the citizens Abe Sylla, President of AIS Engineering, for the support they have given me. I am also indebted to some Guinean executives, including MP Ibrahim Bangoura. I would also like to thank the members of the Guinean press, in particular, the RTG, for the encouraging contribution they have given us.

The dramatic changes I have witnessed in the Soso culture offer inspiration and have pushed me to delve into the vast ensemble of Djalon Soso. Thus, in 1979, I resolved to contribute to documenting the Soso culture. I am convinced that the constructive debates that took place through various radio stations, including Radio Nostalgia, Radio Continentale, RTG and Radio Empire Soso from the USA, have contributed to increasing the importance of the Koré Sèbèli alphabet in our history.

Consequently, I am particularly pleased that we have a book that allows us to get a better idea of different perspectives on our history. I am convinced that the revitalization of the Soso empire based on its cultural values based on the Laga, will help to promote a brighter future. In so much so, our elders worked patiently to expand their spheres of influence to make this book a reality and thus, offer the reassurance of rebuilding the culture of the great Soso Empire. The Soso community thirsts for this information, and this is why I am delighted to document in print form, the authentic values of the Soso culture. It is somewhat difficult and even impossible to document all of the cultural contributions of the Soso civilization; however, our ethnographic research based information recorded here will serve to enhance the knowledge of the reader further.

INTRODUCTION

The Soso Empire stretched from the north of the two loops of Niger, from Senegal to the coast of the Gulf of Guinea. This empire consisted of several ethnic communities. Djalonkés Limbas, Bagas, Temines, Mandés, Nalos, Bassaris, Yolas, Locos, Landoumas, Guerzé, and Tomas in particular populated the Soso empire. After the collapse of the great Soso empire in 1235 as a result of contacts with the outside world, a number of other sub-ethnic groups assimilated to ethnic sub-groups of Upper Guinea and the average of Guinea. History suggests that large blacks (as opposed to pigmes) originate from the Nile valleys.

I maintain that these large Negroes coming from the Nile valleys have found local Palaeo-Nigritics, which are the Djalonkas. These are the people who lived in the mountainous massifs of Fouta Djalon 4000 years before Christ in search of the iron and the precious metals necessary for the needs of their craft of forge; They are scattered across the different regions of West Africa. The name "Djalonké" means inhabitant of mountainous cliffs. This migratory event is common to several other Palaeo-Nigerian communities in West Africa. (Djalonkas, Lebou, Yola, Baga, and Wolof in particular) These paleo-nigritics lived in the caves of these massifs before building cities within the empire. The first kings of the empire took the title of Faris. The discovery made by the CBG, for an environmental study of pottery that dates from 4000 thousand years BC in the region of Boké. Confirms the existence of Djalonsossos on Guinean land since antiquity. For the potters have Boké on the banks of Tinguilinta as far as Tomini in the Gaoual while passing by Labé, speak the Djalonka.

In search of precious metals, these tribes scatter among the four (4) corners of West Africa following the streams which often drains these precious metals. From the high plateaus towards the east, they moved to Kedougou, in the Gambia, notably in the Dinguira and Tanènè Tosokoii, to the south in Sierra Leone in the Falaba to the west in the Kaloum, they are even found in Burkina, But they keep the name Djalonke. The earliest writings that seek to locate their origin in present-day Mali are erroneous An archaeological excavation would establish that the coast and the mountainous massifs of Fouta Djalon have served more as human habitation than the savannah because mountains have always served as Shelter for prehistoric men.

My research shows that the Djalonkes have moved from west to east, keeping the name of the kolatier Kolana tree, while their linked neighbors name the same tree, the "Woro" fruits. The fact that this coastal plant is called Kola indicates that it did not exist in the Savannah, for those who came with the fruit, the Djalonke, retained its old name. It was the Djalonke who moved from west to east, bringing the cola to the Savannah during their migration in search of gold and precious stones.

CHAPTER I: THE Soso EMPIRE

Each of the first three great empires of West Africa below were endowed with a charter:

1- The Empire of Ghana of 790 - 1077: the charter of Koumbi 14 articles;
2- The Empire of Soso of 1077 - 1235: the charter of Kemekiriyah 100 articles;
3- The Empire of Mali from 1235 - 1400: the charter of Kouroukanfouga 44 articles;

Under the leadership of the prestigious founder of the Soso Empire, Emperor Dantuma, Ghana fell in 1077. The Sosos regained its independence and subjected the rest of the kingdoms to the north of the two loops of Niger and Senegal and Dantuma annexed them as part o his empire. The present coastline of Guinea and the Fouta Djalon lay south of Senegal and formed a large part of the Soso Empire by sheltering the capital of Tabon in 1155 in the Labé at the time of the emperor Soso Frigui one of the descendants of Manga Labé Camara. The successive sovereigns succeeded one another on the throne of the Soso Empire, which are:

Soso Dantouma, founder 1077-1109 (32 years of reign)
Soso Wali 1109-1129 (20 years old)
Soso Bouyé 1129-1155 (26 years old)
Soso Frigui 1155-1178 (23 years old)
Soso Yata 1178-1207 (29 years old)
Soso Soumaoro or Dabi Fana Soumah 1207-1235 (28 years old)

In their fighting to dominate and impose themselves on the high plateau, the Soso built a great fortress towards 1055 denominated Guèmèsangan. These dynamic people fought seven major battles:

1- The battle of Kaniyah 1076 against Sarakole
2- The Battle of Tabo in the Labé in 1160 against the Marakha, king of Meme
3- The battle of Kankignè against the Bambaras in 1220 which inhabits the kingdom of Mali
4- The battle of Negebaiyah in 1222 against Dankarantouma
5- The battle of Kirina 1235 against the army of Soundjata or Soumaoro found death.
6- The battle of Niani in 1255 against the army of the Manden empire, from where Soundjata died on the Niani River and was carried by the Djalonkas, led by Manguè Barakha Bangoura.
7- The great battle of Gemesangan delivered against the songhaï of Soni Ali Ber in 1416. Under the direction of the son of Manguè Barakha, the Soso denominated Wali Barakha, who consecrated the victory of the Soso army and defeated the Sonrhaïs.

Soso Antiquity Culture And Civilization

CULTURAL ORGANIZATION

Established in 1077, the Soso emperor Dantouma, reorganized the teaching of the laga or school whose foundations are listed below:

1- Laga = school
2- Soumè = Inspector of Education
3- Kissango or Sango = great master
4- Sema = inspector
5- Kotè = supervisor
6- Mikhigbé = the student
7- Limbi = school uniformity
8- Lambéma = student

The aim of this training school was to shape the perspectives of adult life. Its teaching was endowed with a form of writing called Fendali or Fedakhié, an integration of songs, myths, hunting, combat, figures, history, tales, legends, customs of the Sosso's tradition and various trades. The central features of this teaching is based on the following 12 words:

Gan ———————————————— ⊥

Dera ———————————————— ⊙

Kikeren ———————————————— |

Khousa ———————————————— ⟠

Sansogué ———————————————— ⊣

Sanfindi ———————————————— ⌐

Yafindi ————————————	7
Kofindi ————————————	⌐
Kisango ————————————	✕
Tounkhouma ————————————	⊖
Kirasso ————————————	⌀
Sekan ————————————	⊤

In the Soso laga the names of the great Emperors are known in the form of a coded dialogue.

-Nbegan?
-Dantouma, we add n'houn which means, "and after"
-The initiator or student answers Sansogué 'khounsa.
-The Kissango, great master, returns to the charge:
-Nbedèra? Wali khounsa dera
-Nbé khounsa? Bouyé khounsa kofindi
-Nbekikeren? Frigui khounsa sansogué
-Nosansogue? Yata khounsa kirasso
-Nbé sanfindi? Soumaoro khounsa tounkhouma

As mentioned previously, the infamous fortress of Guèmèsangan, remains, and still considered a legend in the history and the resistance of the Soso people. Its looming structure has endured successive empires. The fortress remains impenetrable and invincible, until the fall of the last empire of Africa of The west. This explains why the coast of Africa or the coast of Guinea have not been subjected to either the Manden domination or to the kings of Sonrhai. From Guinea-Bissau to Sierra Leone, the coastal peoples, in particular, the Sosos, the Ashantis, Nigeria, and Benin, have always retained their autonomy as great conquerors of people. The Laga, which is the incontestable cultural element of the history of the Sosos, is translated as "LA," meaning "Faith" or trust. The Soussou believe in "La n'na"; a belief in God or "will imariguira." "GA," also translated as a beginning, or another denomination of God.

Soso Antiquity Culture And Civilization

Thus, the school of faith and the beginning set the stage because its contact with this school established the foundation of learning and a new life for man. Laga is not only a school of life, but also a school of the knowledge of God. Civilizing missions distinguish the peculiarity and formulation of a "Cultural Identity" of the Soso people, and whose mysteries are forbidden to anthropologists and foreign historians.

Today, thanks to a research of 30 years, we penetrated this icy ocean of immortal knowledge. According to the teachings of the Laga, people who do not preserve their culture condemn themselves to dissimilar their qualities in another culture more conservative and thus eventually disappear.

After the fall of the empire, teachers called Sémas took charge of transmitting to the new generations the ways of organizing their society thanks to a series of formations given through the 12 words that define the Sosokas (Sosos Communities) Differentiate it from other neighboring communities. Thus, in Soso countries, the 12 words are declared to make themselves understood. Hence the adage: "When the child provides the effort, his father offers him the 12 gifts. Like the 12 tribes that God gave to Israel and 12 months to mankind, He gives 12 specific words to the Sosos peoples for their covenant. The Sosos have developed a calendar that begins with the days, months, years and century, as follows:

The seven-seventh days of the week: Lakhati, Tenen, Talatè, Meta, Tanmè, Fo-inti and Simiti. The 12 months of the year: Libiti, Ferefouna, Doundoulenyi, Lèbèrè bèrè, Linlinyi, Lambè, Figui-Figui, Sansanyi, Barakha, Falè, Soura, Khabidonyi.

Before the foundation of their empire in 1077, the Sosos lived on a territory situated between mountains and denominated Djalen; which explains the name Djalonkas, inhabitants of Djalen. At the establishment of their empire, the Sosos name their first Emperor, Dantouma Sekan Wouli kikeren. The Dantouma of 1001 years and their second emperor in the Laga, called the Wali Seken wouli Sansogué khounsa or wali 1032, and their last ruler, called Manguè Séken wouli Kikeren. By definition, Yafindi Tounkhouma means, the king of the year 1158. For oral and practical purposes, the estimated year is calculated to be, 1939 of the Soso calendar. In pragmatic terms, this corresponds to the year, 2016 of the Greek calendar. Explicitly, the year "77" of the Greek calendar coincided with that the Soso people, and it was in this same year that the Soso invented their calendar. They subsequently constituted their charter and named it, "Charter of Kèmèkiriyah," in 1077 of the Greek calendar, and 1001 years of the Soso calendar.

This document predicted in their school of knowledge that the world would experience a great change in the year 9000, Tounkhouma sarama Seken wouli kirasso, and according to their calendar, there remain 6261 years of great upheaval to follow. However, the Sosos did not talk about the end of the world, like the Mayan calendar, but rather the upset of normal life cycles.

B - The LAGA: (the Black School)

The Laga is composed of two (2) words: This signifies La n'na, that is, believe in my existence, implies the idea of belief in God. GA which means the beginning (God) of Fendali elements.

According to the Sossokas in their sacred book called WAKARA preserved for thousands of years explains these: creation began with light or fire, then air then water and finally the earth after followed the appearance Of man. In detail they say Kouyé nou i foro (the atmosphere was obscure), then light that means yalan illuminates Kouye to become kouyé yalanyi, which is light. And GAN is the beginning. This light means knowledge or knowledge. In other words, for the Wakarakas, in the beginning there was darkness or darkness, then light has invaded the darkness, and man has become conscious of his own existence, he is enlightened. So the Laga is the school of belief in a beginning, and therefore that of knowledge.

1 - THE LEGEND:

Soso originates from combining two words, Djalonka So: meaning entrance and So: which means horse. In essence the city takes in the horses.

Warrior invaders who repulsed the pigmees of equatorial Africa and elsewhere in the Savannah were founders of the first great cities in antiquity, such as Tabou, Tamba, Kounkouba, and Farinta. Before the main cities of the Empire of Ghana were Tombouctou and Walata. The Sosos Djalons practiced crafts such as pottery, blacksmithing, weaving, hunting, and agriculture. With the advent of the empire in 1077, the Sosos founded new towns in the following areas: Galita (Kirina and its surroundings), Khunkhouba in its forest, its center, Macenta; Solima Tamba (Niani and surrounding areas); Djalon (Tabou and surrounding areas); Khaloum (Guème sangan); Khan mousiga and Tambacounda. The Djalonkas existed from the high plateaus of Fouta to the littoral, and now its current name, Siguiri mud.

2 New Kingdom (1236 - 1450)

Limits of the Soso Empire in 1236, after the battle of Kirina posed some challenges, as well as complicit agreements with some of the Djalonkes. The Kirina rebellion divided the territory in two, and under the authority of Sundiata, the dissidents occupied the eastern regional areas, from Timbuktu to Bagaya, now known currently as, Dabola. From Dabola to the Coast of Africa, the Sosos reject invasion by rival groups. In their expansion, they went on to form various territories under the direction of King Simba Kondon Bangoura. He was the legitimate heir to Soumaoro in 1236, whose capital was Thia, currently known as Boffa. King Bangoura married his wife Wondé Keleya, the daughter of his younger brother Fakoly, who bore him a son named Kankou Keleya.

In 1236, the territory occupied by the dissidents which extend from Timbuktu to Bagaya took the name of the land of the son of Makhan after their meeting in Kourkanfouga. Makhaden or by defamation, Maden. In Africa, the following words are often used in the diminutive: to say Momodouba, we say Momo. To say, Souleyman, they say Souley. Makhaden, it is said to be "Maden." Maden is the name of the Emperor of Mali Sundiata, who was the son of Makhan the liberator of the territory that bore his name after the battle of Kirina, in 1235.

By 1240, Sundiata suspected the valiant warriors Djalonkas of wanting to oust him. He made a plan to eliminate them and forbid their speaking of the Djalonke language. This strategy, it is said, undermined the warriors of Djalonkas, and is an oral documentation of how Kamandjan Camara and many warriors of the Djalonkas were murdered. Oral tradition indicates that in 1250, one the Djalonka warriors, Fakoly escaped death and joined forces with the Soso in their attempt to recover their lost territory. Following the death of Fakoly, another fighter, Kandet Barakha assumed leadership. He regained control of the area and resorted to changing the name from Kaya and changing its name to Manguè Barakha. Following their victory, the Sosos mobilized all the African coast and the counties of Fouta Djalon and all neighboring communities such as Kognaguis, Bassaris, Temines, Bagas, Lokos, Landoumas, and Badjarankés. Regions which bore Djalonke names occupied the mountainous massifs of Djalon and took part in the battle of Niani. This amalgamation of forces represents one of the biggest armies known in West Africa history. According to legend, in 1255, the troops of the Sossokas attacked Sundiata in Niani with nearly 30 thousand warriors. The Djalonkes inflicted heavy damaged to armies of Sundiata. Legend has it that his opponents take his body to Badjar. It is an explanation that the return of the warrior chief Barakha body, remain in the memories and often celebrated by the camp of Barakhayayé.

These oral traditions are held in high regards and recognize the king's reign, which lasted for sixty years. Barakha ruled the Soso kingdom from the west, until 1310. His body was carried in a hurry, where it is said, they lost his head. At the age of twenty years old, Bakhara assumed leadership, where he lived and ruled for four eight decades. Upon his death, in 1310, Woula Soumah took Bakhara's place and ruled until 1360. However, in 1360 when, Woula Soumah died, Domi Conté assumed his role as leader, and reigned until 1410. His nephew, Kandet Barakha, subsequently took control and rebuilt the Guèmèsangan barrier. However, under Kandet's rule, in 1410, the Sonni Ali Beri's Songhai army attacked his army, and almost defeated the Sossokas. With the help of an army of mercenaries fighting by his side, and commanded by Koly Tenguéla, from the north (Senegal) and a strategic war plan, using first wave attacks of the animist Peulhs in the Fouta Djalonke, the Sossokas prevailed.

Thanks to the Guèmèsangan barrier, the Soso kingdom remains impenetrable. In 1450, one of the nephews of Barakha, Woula Katty the dominated and took over power. The apogee of the empire and its ultimate fragmentation created several sub-kingdoms in the 15th and 16th centuries resulting in the slave trade. Yari Gbéli an empress warrior, aka (Red Yari from BAKIYA in the Bouramaya) organized a powerful army to fight men hunters on the coast to Fariya in Boffa. Article 26 of Kememiriyah, stipulates that any sale not subjected to the testimony of a king or localities is considered a provocation of war. Article 26 helps to reduce the depopulation of the coast to the confines of the high plateau of Fouta. In the middle of the 18th century, revolts broke out in various Gulf of Guinea kingdoms against trafficking. An army of kingdoms mobilizes against European robbers. European governments and some Western philanthropists are committed to ending the slave trade. Having set the tone, England is followed by other countries. However, the arrival of a second wave of the Peulhs in the Fouta in the eighteenth century leaving the east found refuge with the Djalonkes, who offered them hospitality. Some years later, they established friendly relations with the neighbors of the Djalonke, who are the Musak Marakas and Yakankes. Those cis having kept the hatred of the defeat of 1060 in Labé at the time of king Frigui who had for capital Tabo; Soon made an alliance with the Muslim Fulhs to seize power in the current Timbo Tabo. The Djalonkés, surprised at the declaration of war, were unable to register, and then Chief Djalonke and his troops rejoined their parents at Faranah in Marela, Danda, others in the Koukoure, and some found refuge at the loan of their parents Sosos.

After the battle of Talansan in 1725, the Peulh seized power and subjected the Diakankes and Djalonkes to the payment of the tax and removed them to the exercise of power. The Diakankes were felt betrayed, for the agreement of the alliance had not been respected. All the diwal were represented by the Peulhs with the title Thierno or Alpha. Well before this period in the eighteenth century, the coast flourished triangular trade and the Sosos crossed the Fouta even in the savannah to sell the salt, the cola and junk that they received from the Portuguese and Dutch traders.

Our research indicates that the areas from Khouré Mali to Koliyah through Tambacounda to Falaba where the Sierra Leone dalons celebrated the Kaya of the year 1937 of the Soso calendar (2014 of the Greek calendar) are inhabited by the djallonke. In other words, the migratory movement referred to is mixed, that is to say; It depicts both the group Djalonkés who leaves a locality leaving other djallonkés on the spot, to join other groups Djallonkés formerly established. It is therefore a looped migration in the same circle. In other words, Guinea is a Jallonke country and explicitly Soso.

C - MILITARY ORGANIZATION

The Sosokas in Article 8 of their charter recommend the defense of the homeland. This is why they focus on teaching young initiates who seek war training during LAGA training cycles. The great masters directed these young people according to the vocations they deserved following a sustained observation during the performance of their various activities. The formation of the being being at the center of the preoccupation of the elders, the young initiate oriented in the body of the warriors undergoes a categorical discipline to form by making him obedient and able to keep the secret of his peers. In the history of the Soso the army was divided in two and included the piroguier and the land combatants. The discovery and mastery of iron from blast furnaces and the introduction of large-scale metallurgical centers which enable them to equip themselves with iron weapons: spears, hunting rifles, cutters, swords and so many other tools. war.

The Sosokas were formidable; According to legend the first Emperor Soso was guarded by 7000 warriors, a tradition that survived until Soumaoro. The military corps consisted of the following 14 ranks: 1 - Gamba; 2 - Dereba; 3 - Kérenba; 4 - Khounba; 5 - Sanguo; 6 - Sanfin; 7 - Yanfin; 8 - Khonba; 9 - Kisanba; 10 - Tounkhounba; 11 - Simba; 12 - Koly; 13 - Baramè; And 14 - Barantan. Our research establishes the veracity of the existence of these different bodies, in particular the example of Galimanguè Sango, Bala Gambanya; Galimanguè Simba and Galimanguè Fakoly.

D - ADMINISTRATIVE ORGANIZATION:

The empire was subject to a highly structured executive whose members were ordinarily from the war hierarchy. The choice of the emperor was submitted to the council of the named. Kountigui whose assembly, assisted him in ruling.

3 - Santigui is a noble warrior who often ordinarily rewarded a position within the executive after his war service to coordinate specific activities. For example, Galisantigui is in charge of defense matters.
4 - Khali also exercises authority at the grassroots level as carrying out key recommendations from the court.
5 - Batoula is an element which plays the role of civil servant in the application of different activities; He accompanies the executive in all departments, particularly in the field of interpreting and similar services.
6 - Kountigui is form the class of the council of sages and represent the different communities that make up the empire. They keep customs and traditions. Their influence allows them to choose the right leader for their communities in the event of a vacancy in power; Often decide during the Kayas the supreme instances of decisions or the choice of a leader, that is why this assembly is called Kaya which means to know oneself. The Kountiguis are distributed as follows:

Santiguigbé chair the sessions;
Santiguis: represent the different communities.

7 - The Firi-Firi Wagabida (High Imperial Council)
They are composed of people in charge of different functions as follows:
Wagas: are those who take care of the king's house (baptisms, weddings)
Wade: takes care of the funeral rites

Waki: takes care of teaching
Wakhoun: takes care of the parents and allies of the king
Wassan: is interested in the king's conjugal life
Wafi: are those who are interested in custody of kings
Waya: is interested in the king's dress
The Wako: are responsible for seeking or choosing doctors, healers for the court
Les Wago: are the storytellers
Watou: are responsible for providing vital information for the king
The Wassos: are advised of war
The Wakan: are the territorial advisers
The Wayens: are the great communicators the latter are often responsible for communicating the latest decisions and his speeches.

The Kakiwondi are chosen from among the best initiated following their competence of the teachings received during the initiation.

Generally in remote periods, women and men stayed several years in the Laga to learn the different trades. Once the return is announced by the kakilambé a number of insiders are selected to take over and these are the ones called kakiwondi.

On returning from the village, their disappearance is announced by placing a calabash in front of their respective parents' huts. In the village, they are considered as martyrs who found the dead during the series of hard tests. And yet, in reality, they are not dead. They are chosen as future priests to serve the universe and soul of ancestors. They do not marry. Practices were abolished and abandoned following the penetration of Christianity and Islam. If they died after the services rendered, they are buried in the great forests under the Baobab (kiri) and are replaced by the future initiates. The opportunity for them to see the village, they will be put in mission, to come to transmit the preaching about the title of kakilambé, without being recognized by the parents during the great ceremonies. After the ceremonies, he returned to the great forest, joined the college of kakiwondis.

kakilambé's priests are recognized by all the Sossoka communities, namely the Jalon Soso, Limbanyi, Landouma, Baga, Nalo, Mandenyi, Yola and several other ethnic sub-groups that share almost the same traditional values.

E - LEGAL ORGANIZATION:

The Soso people had adopted a charter after the breakup of Ghana, in order to thwart the Almoravids who wished to conquer all of West Africa to make it an empire under the slogan of Islamization. Thus, in 1077, during a Kaya in Kirina, located between the prefectures of Mali and Tougué, which borders the Republic of Mali in its western part, Manguè Fory Dantouma founded an empire to defend the Soso territory against the invaders Almoravides and safeguard its cultural values.

The Kaya to which reference is made below is the higher decision-making body supported by the general assembly of representatives of the different Sossokas communities. In 1077, under the tree kiri baobab they agreed on 100 items to regulate their living conditions.

CHAPTER II: The Charter of KEMEKIRIYAH

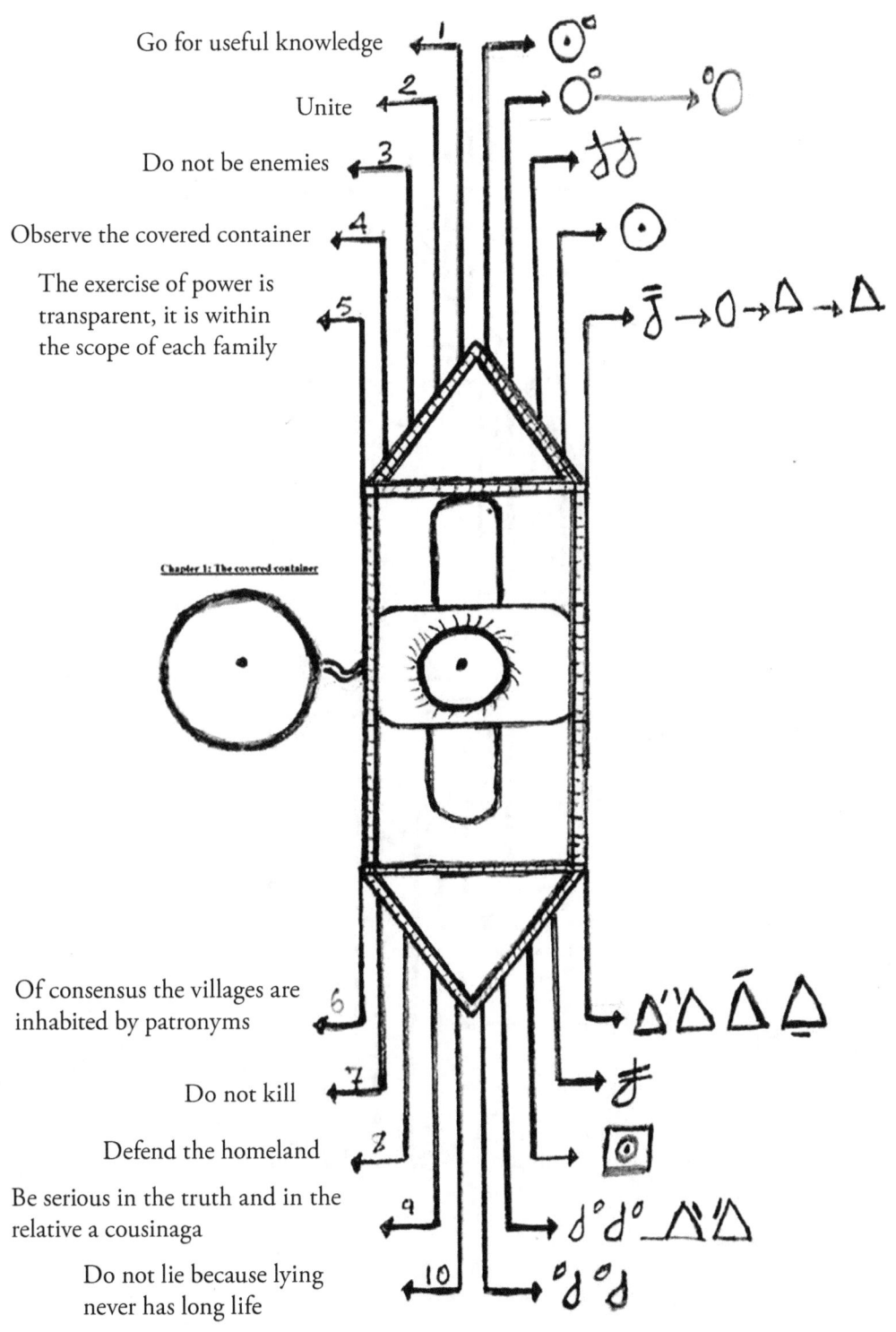

The act is sacred, it is defeated only by another pact

Do not steal

Seek the blessing of your parents

Save the homeland

Do not commit adultery

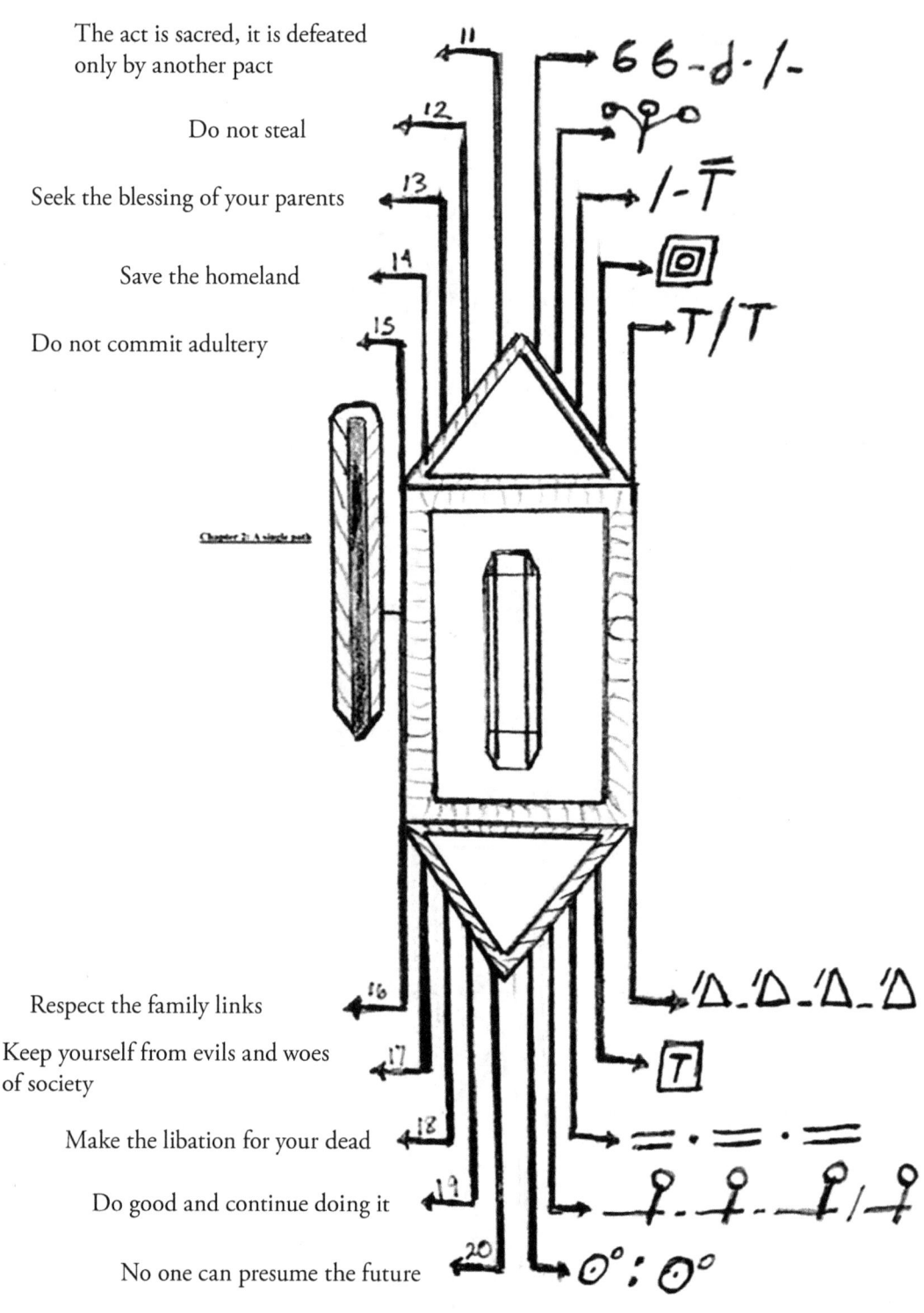

Chapter 2: A single path

Respect the family links

Keep yourself from evils and woes of society

Make the libation for your dead

Do good and continue doing it

No one can presume the future

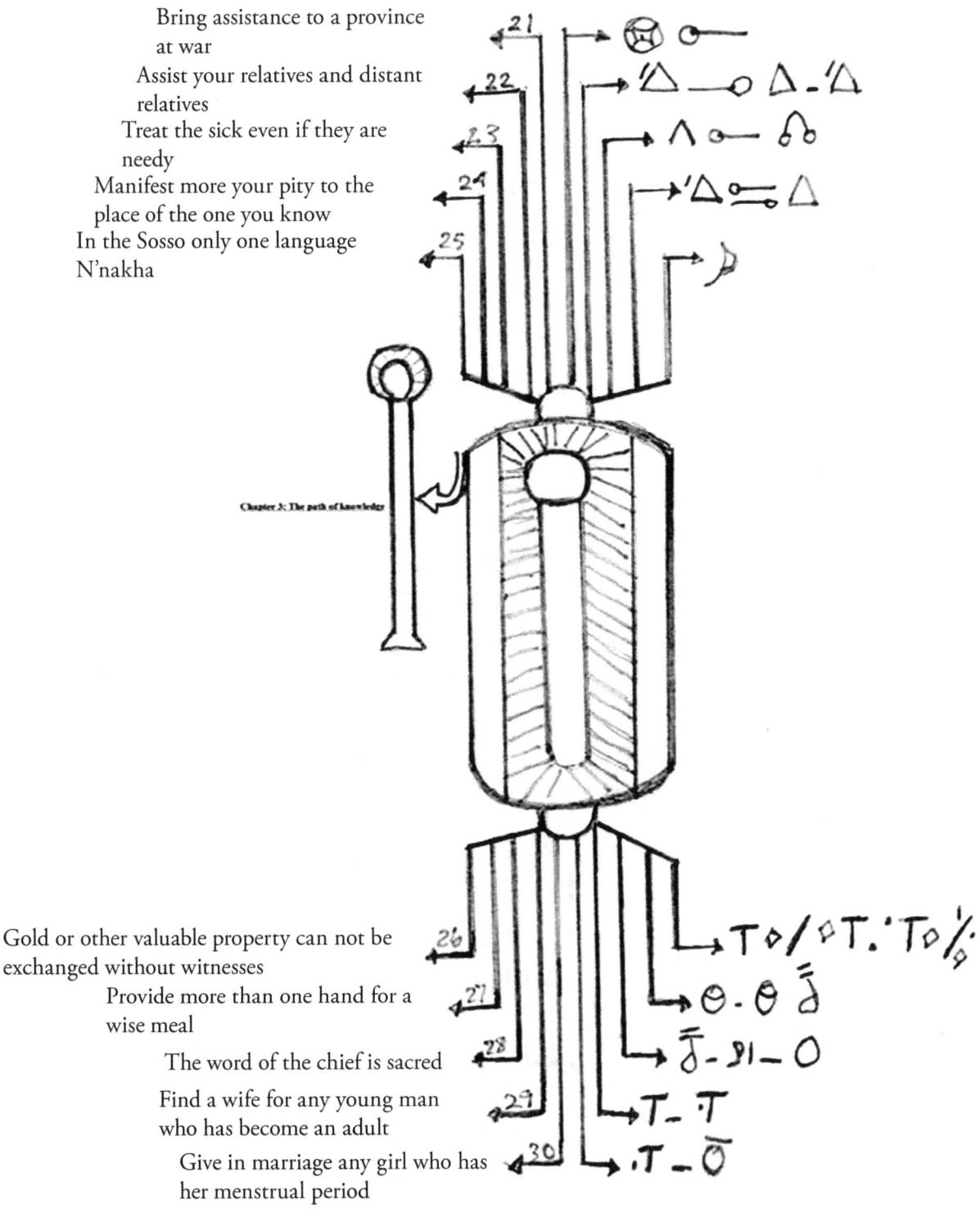

Bring assistance to a province at war
Assist your relatives and distant relatives
Treat the sick even if they are needy
Manifest more your pity to the place of the one you know
In the Sosso only one language N'nakha

Chapter 3: The path of knowledge

Gold or other valuable property can not be exchanged without witnesses
Provide more than one hand for a wise meal
The word of the chief is sacred
Find a wife for any young man who has become an adult
Give in marriage any girl who has her menstrual period

Soso Antiquity Culture And Civilization

Do not pick fruit before maturity

Every village must have its military camp

Know that destiny is variable (yesterday, today and tomorrow

The boundaries of the province can be either mountains, rivers, or extended spaces etc...

The hunter is obliged to bring back to the village his game

In case of crisis, the word comes back to the wise

The young people carry out the commissions and report

In case of conflicts, all ages are mobilized

Do not recruit an enemy in the army

Work for a better tomorrow

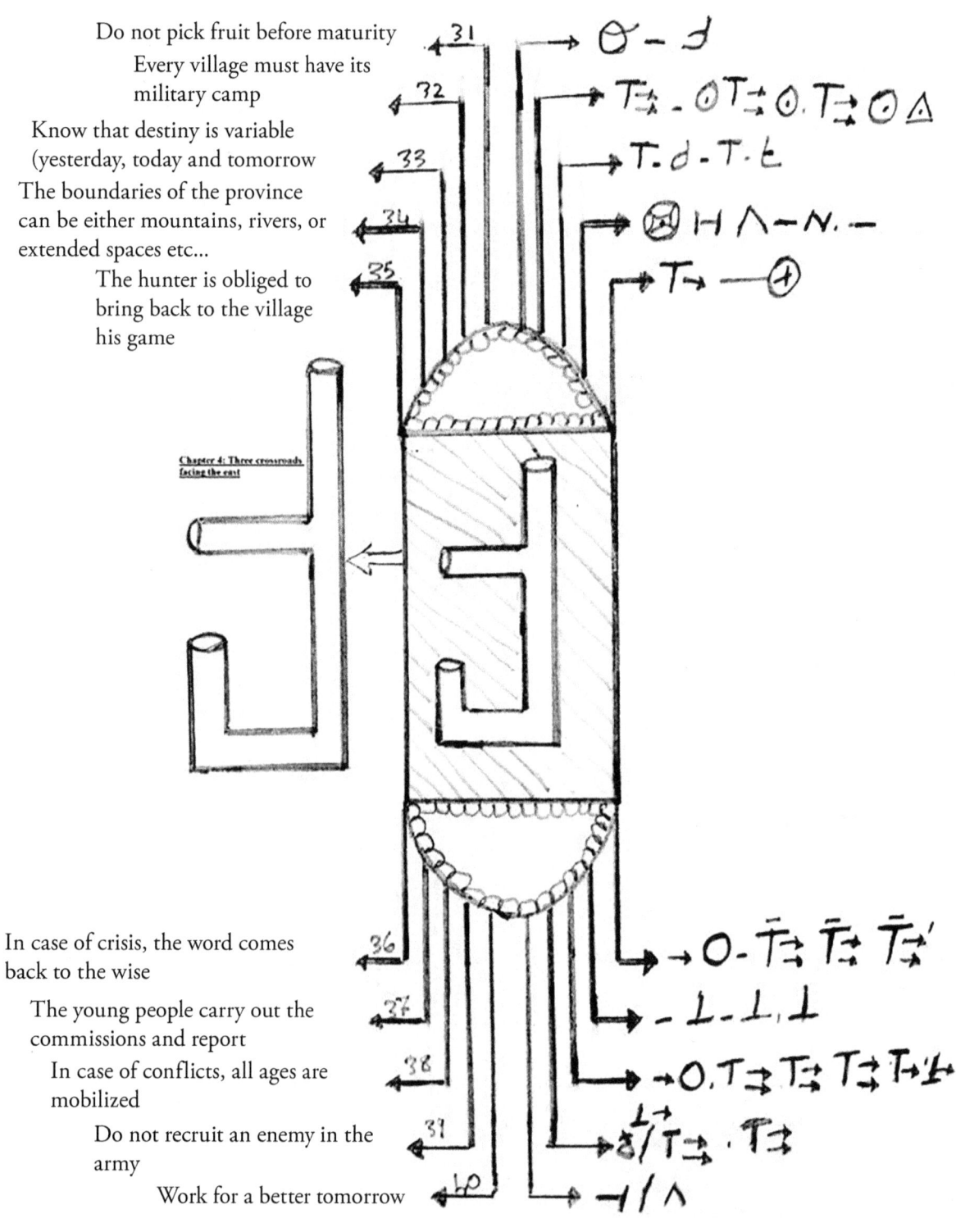

Chapter 4: Three crossroads facing the east

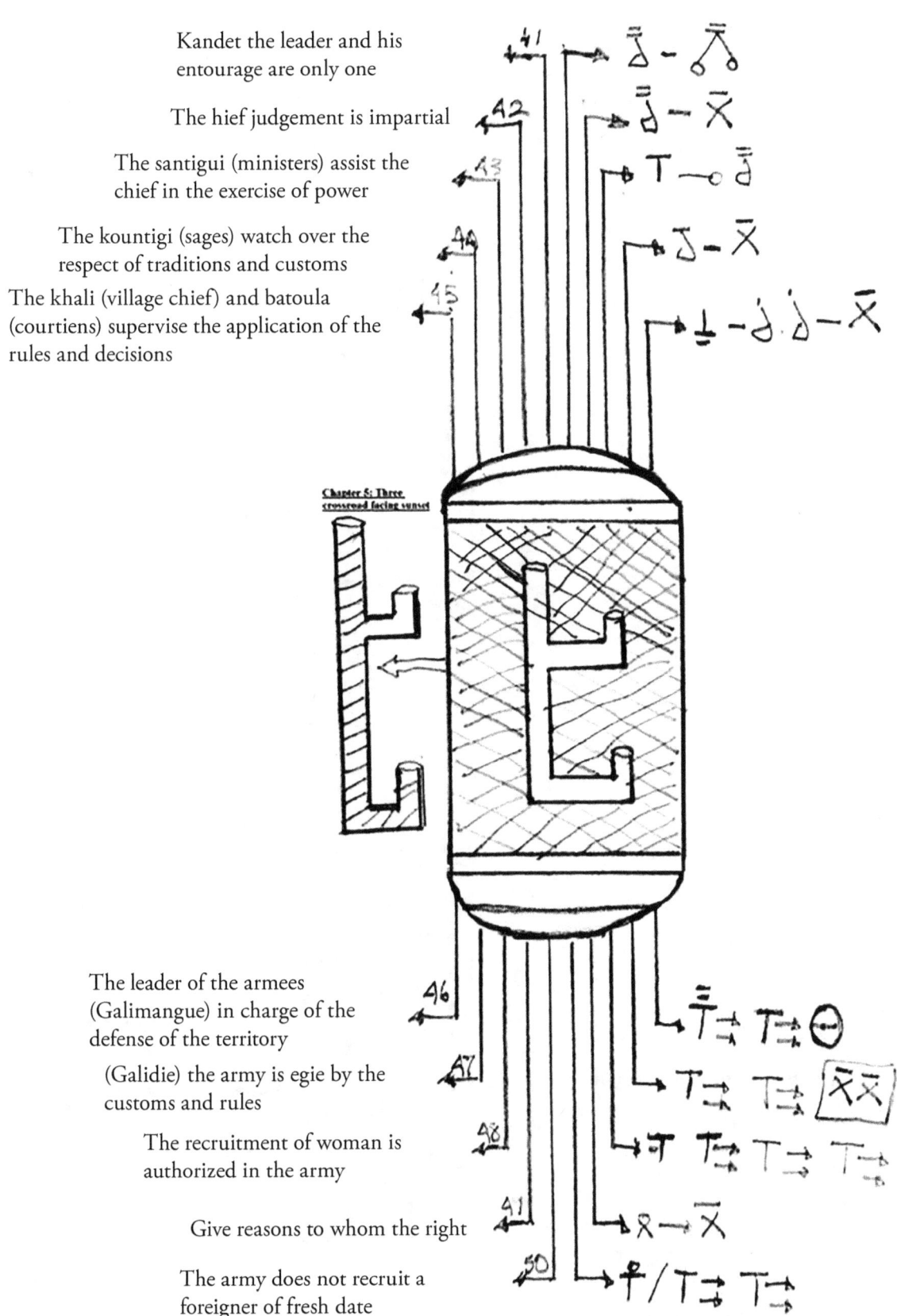

Kandet the leader and his entourage are only one

The hief judgement is impartial

The santigui (ministers) assist the chief in the exercise of power

The kountigi (sages) watch over the respect of traditions and customs

The khali (village chief) and batoula (courtiens) supervise the application of the rules and decisions

Chapter 5: Three crossroad facing sunset

The leader of the armees (Galimangue) in charge of the defense of the territory

(Galidie) the army is egie by the customs and rules

The recruitment of woman is authorized in the army

Give reasons to whom the right

The army does not recruit a foreigner of fresh date

Soso Antiquity Culture And Civilization

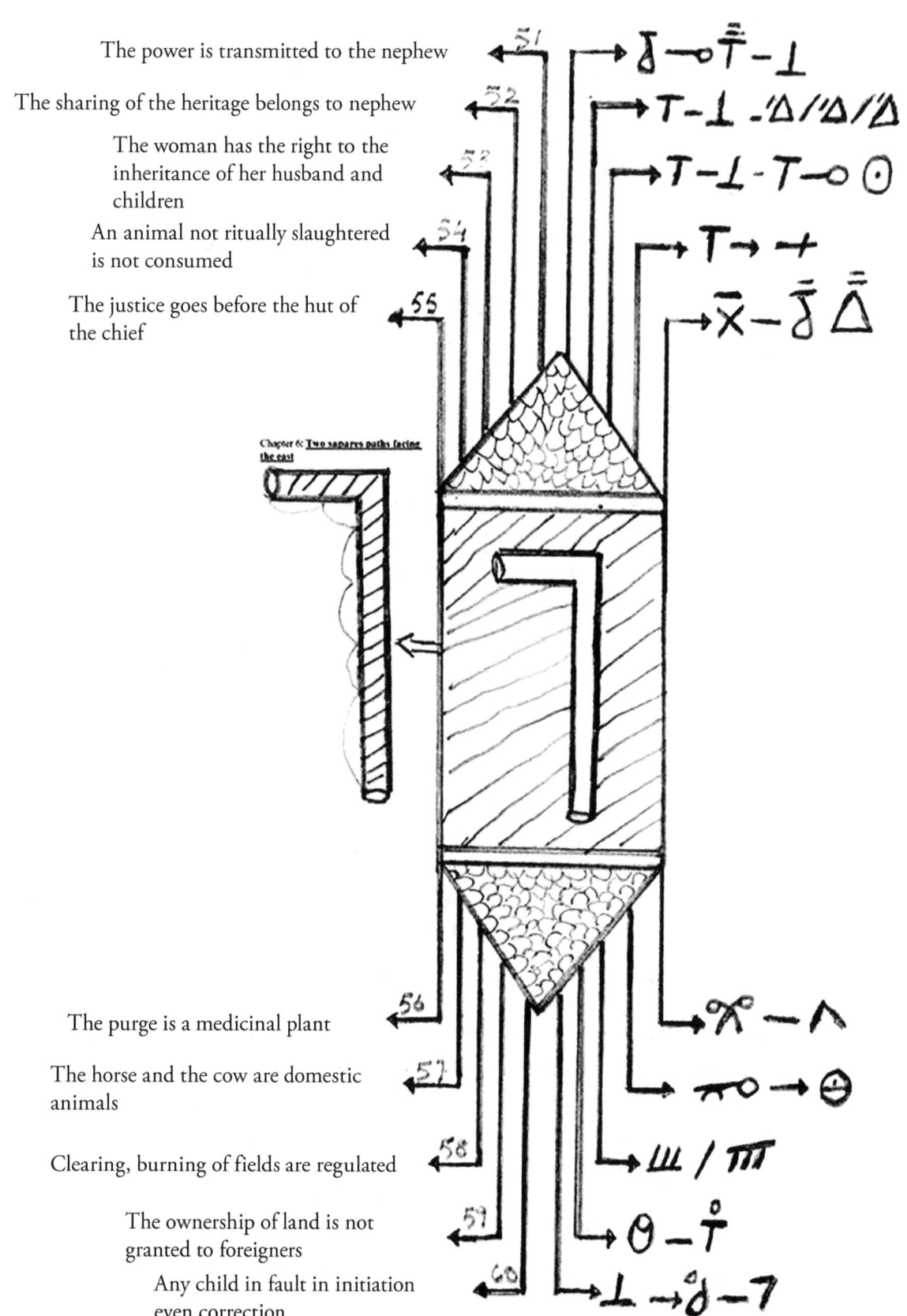

Mohamed Bentoura Bangoura

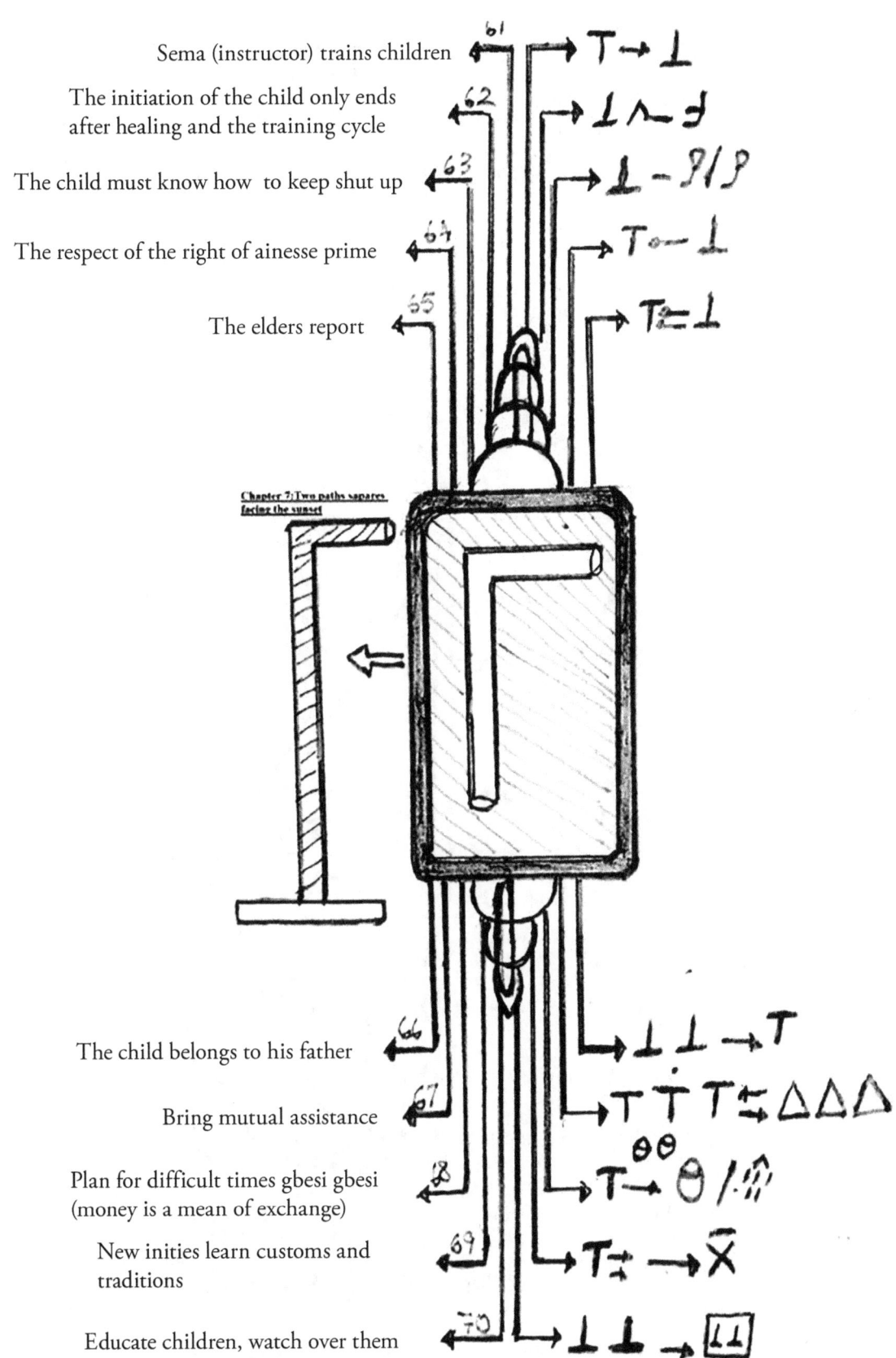

Sema (instructor) trains children

The initiation of the child only ends after healing and the training cycle

The child must know how to keep shut up

The respect of the right of ainesse prime

The elders report

The child belongs to his father

Bring mutual assistance

Plan for difficult times gbesi gbesi (money is a mean of exchange)

New inities learn customs and traditions

Educate children, watch over them

Soso Antiquity Culture And Civilization

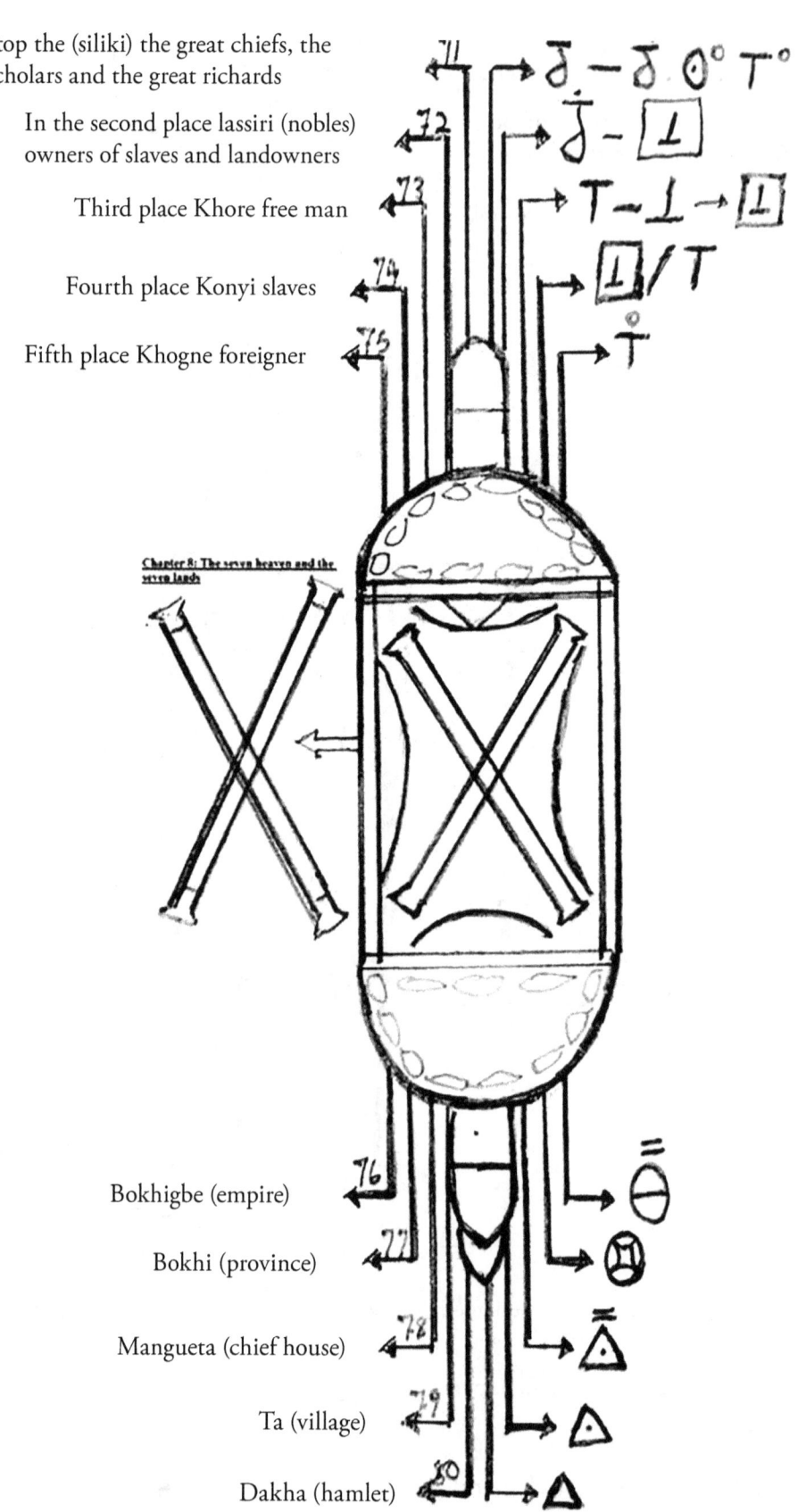

To thetop the (siliki) the great chiefs, the great scholars and the great richards

In the second place lassiri (nobles) owners of slaves and landowners

Third place Khore free man

Fourth place Konyi slaves

Fifth place Khogne foreigner

Bokhigbe (empire)

Bokhi (province)

Mangueta (chief house)

Ta (village)

Dakha (hamlet)

No village bears the name of a foreigner

The ight to asylum is devoted to

Divorce is prohibited

Slaves, women and children are not responsible for their actions

The hief's house is the highest in the capital

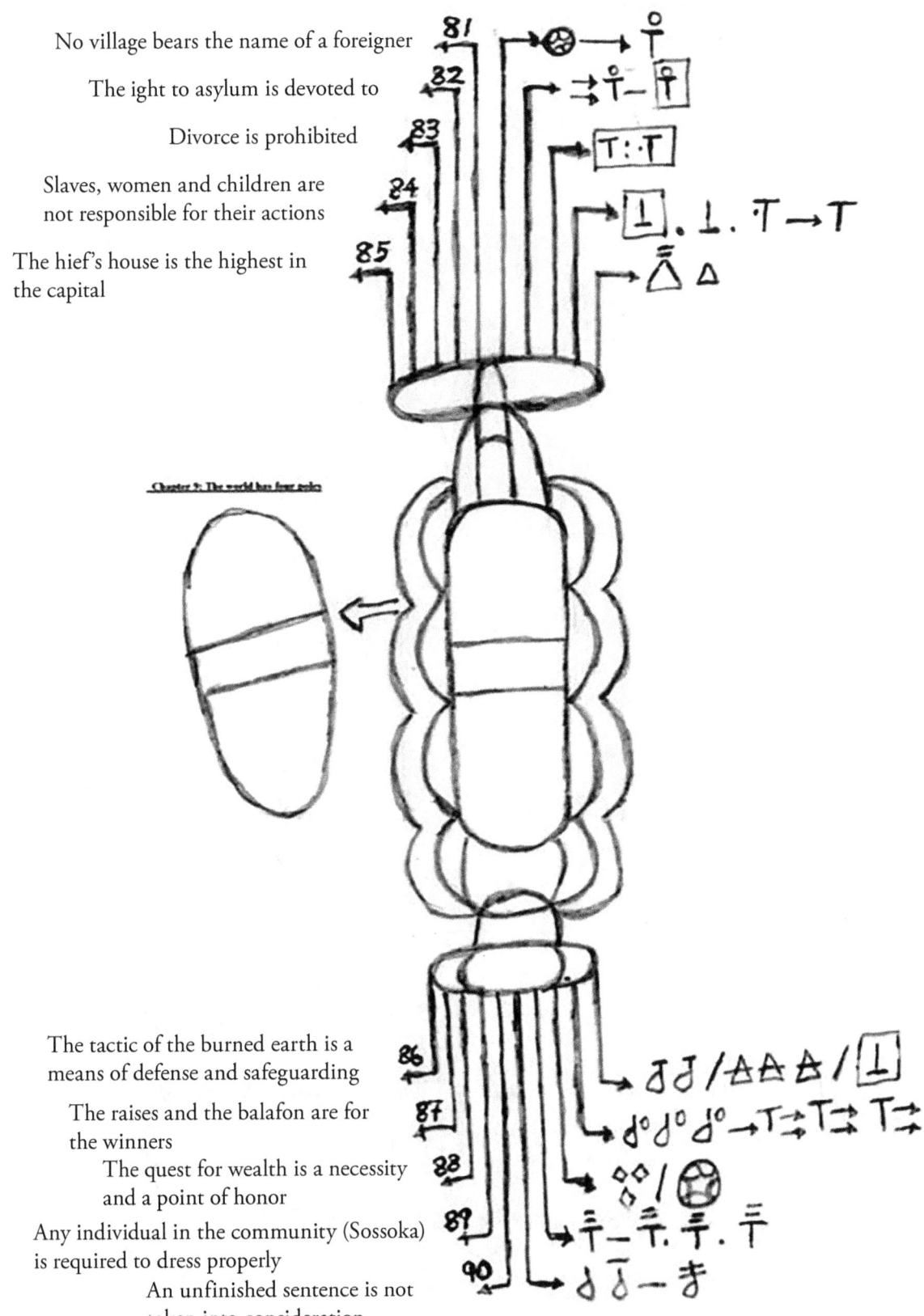

Chapter 9: The world has four poles

The tactic of the burned earth is a means of defense and safeguarding

The raises and the balafon are for the winners

The quest for wealth is a necessity and a point of honor

Any individual in the community (Sossoka) is required to dress properly

An unfinished sentence is not taken into consideration

Soso Antiquity Culture And Civilization

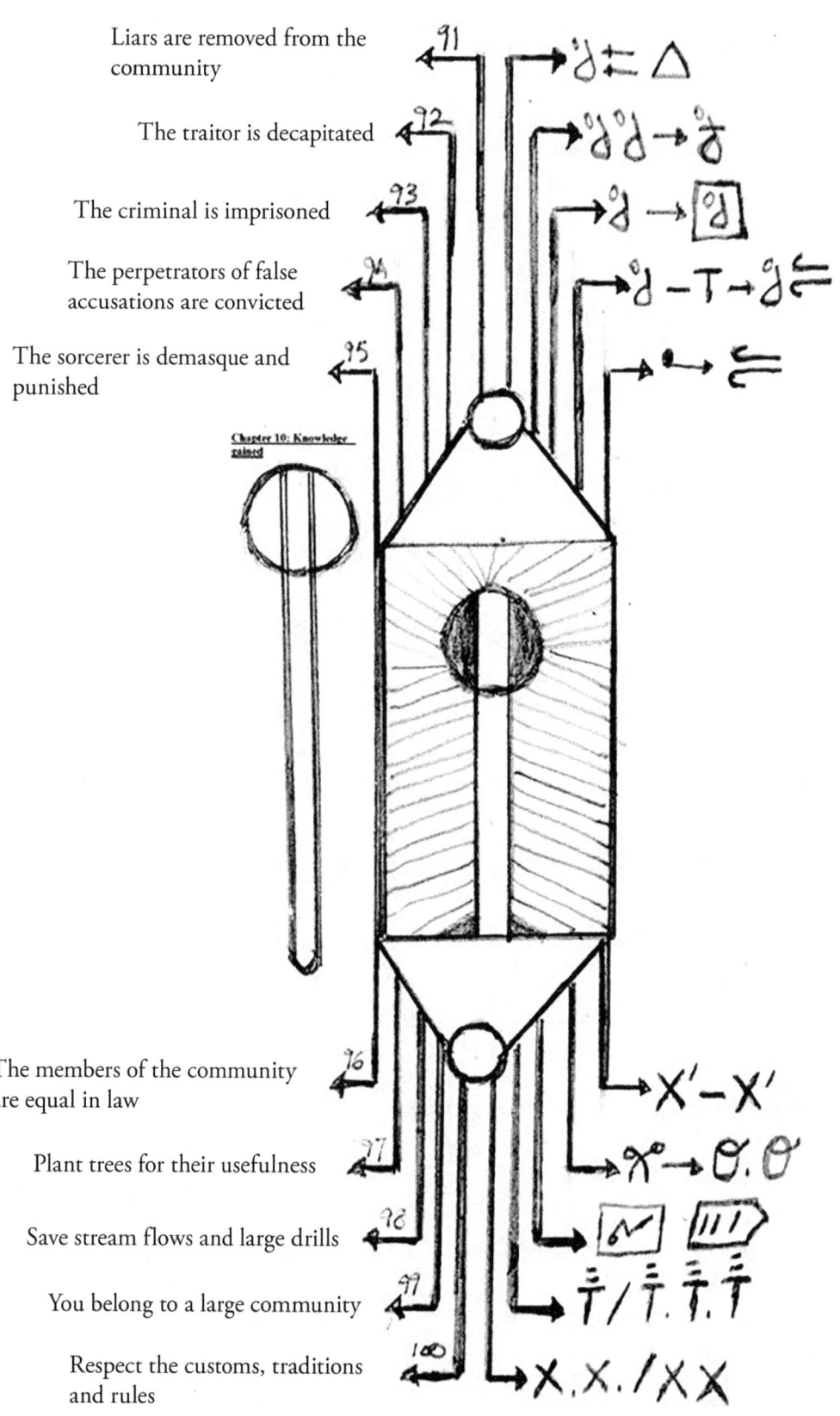

Liars are removed from the community

The traitor is decapitated

The criminal is imprisoned

The perpetrators of false accusations are convicted

The sorcerer is demasque and punished

The members of the community are equal in law

Plant trees for their usefulness

Save stream flows and large drills

You belong to a large community

Respect the customs, traditions and rules

Mohamed Bentoura Bangoura

Chapter III: Explanation of the Twelve FEDALI Signs

GAN: is the first sign of the twelve alphabetical signs, it means beginning. The beginning is the darkness, which is to the knowledge of the master of the universe called 'koyé Mangué', that is why he swears in the name of Gan, saying "Khamunaki Gan" which means, that I return to the beginning. To give importance to the beginning Gan, he names his mother N'ga or the name of the woman N'Gandé, the place of my departure, in the womb of his mother.

This hieroglyphic sign is of great capital importance, for in order to consult the scrapers, it means a light, a flame if this is drawn by lot, the interested one can hope on to achieve these objectives. It is also used to differentiate between cattle since antiquity, it can be used on the construction of huts, to attract happiness in the hearth or against square unhappiness.

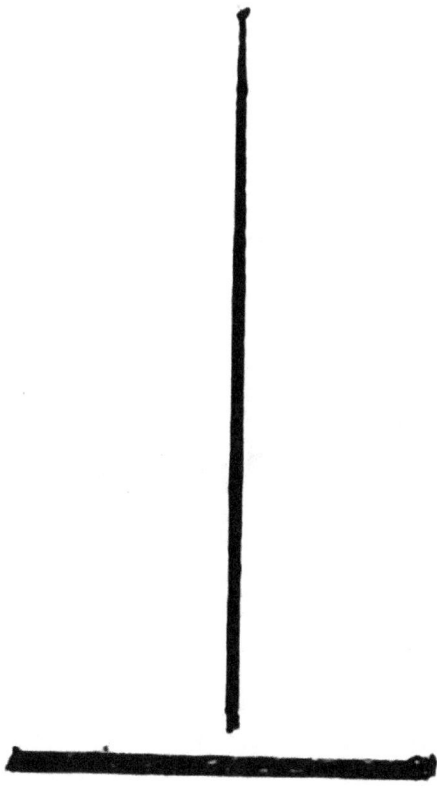

DERA: is the sign of the twelve hyroglyphic figures called "fendani". According to the Sosos in laga, this sign is the source of the formation of the universe. It is the myth of the center of the universe. It represents coagulated blood, and the formation of planets. This sign is of paramount importance in the interpretation of the facts. It represents the divine eye, which watches the whole world and also equivalent to the power of controlling living beings everywhere. This figure brings happiness that is why it is used to the construction of huts for habitation, and also in the kitchens of the affluent men. According to tradition, this sign prevents harm in households.

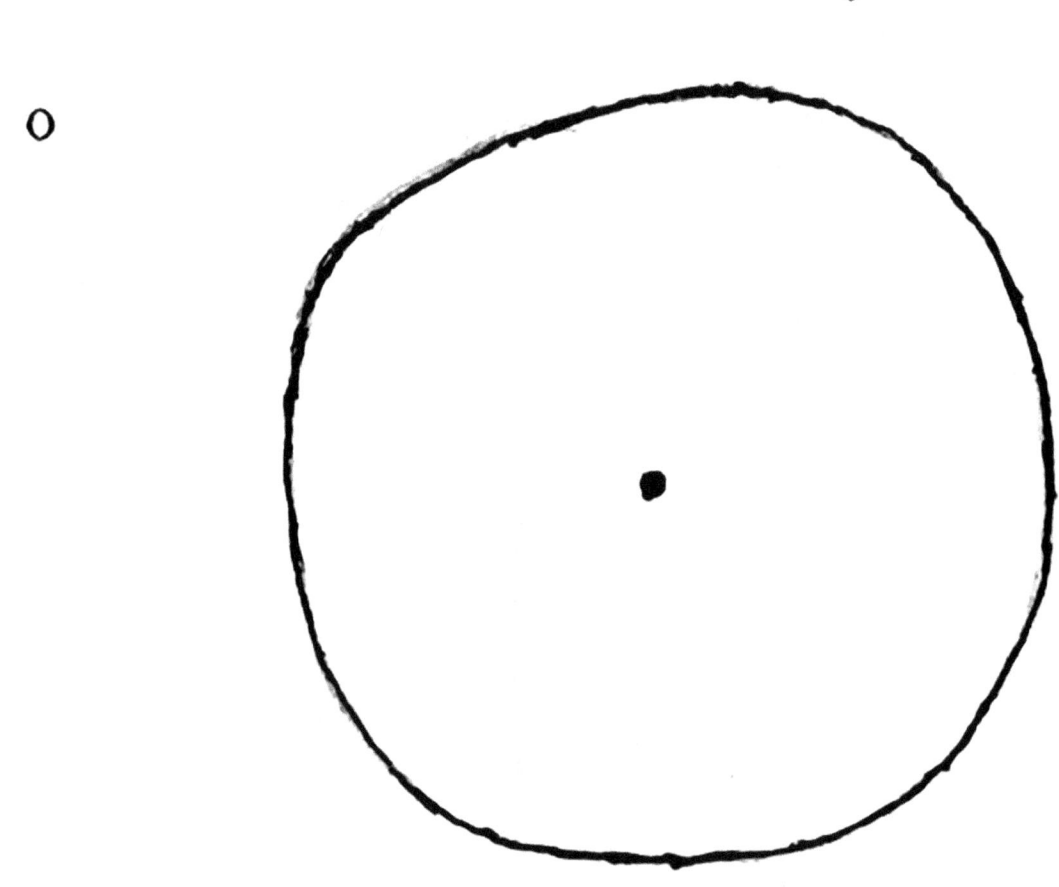

KIKEREN: is the third sign of the twelve hyroglyphs, demonstrating the path of knowledge, for an initiate the path of knowledge is its objective to know the fendalis. It is the way of virtue that explains what a man must learn. He must be just, honest, learn and apply correctly, the principles and rules of laga.

This sign was also used between a young boy and a girl. When the two young friends are together, it is considered a sacred sign. Once placed between the two people, they will not commit adultery. This sign serves to initiate men by putting both hands on the sign and swear truthfully.

KHOUNSA : means the path that goes towards the laga (the school) it is taught to the initiates to put in their future person and progeniture in the school. Often this sign demonstrates the importance of knowledge, which is the compass of the human being. It is also used by men to differentiate animals. A faith in the village that a person reaches an advanced age, who placed him above everyone, his hut was bandaged to the deventure by this sign, to show that it is the wisest of the village and that its Gives him respect and humility, and respectability on the part of the inhabitants of the village.

SANSOGUE:

This sign is three roads that faces the east. It demonstrates that there are three ways.

1- The path of truth,
2- The path of the lie,
3- The path of invisibility.

The sign teaches that the first two paths can all lead man towards his goal, but they have different ways of getting there. However, he who initiates the first path, chooses the way of truth.

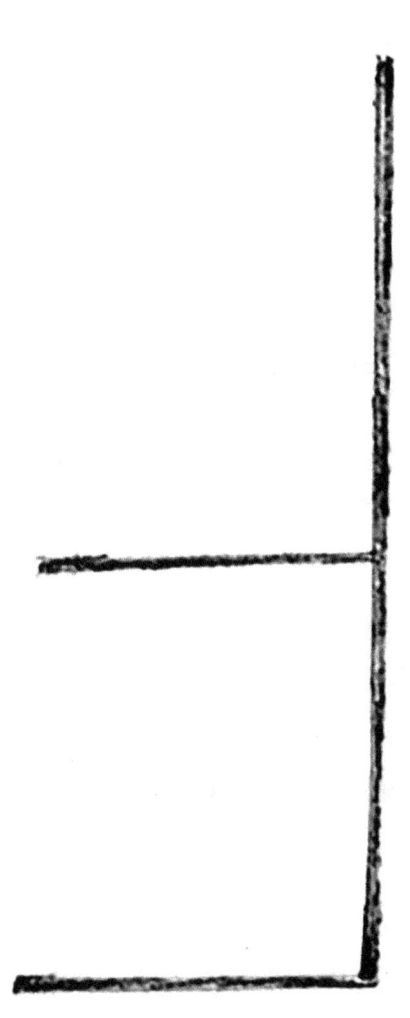

SANFINDI : is the opposite of SANSOGUE. It does not apply to the principles of truth, or brings regret. Using it incorrectly can be also dangerous and may cause undue stress to the user. Initiates are instructed to choose only path of truth, which leads to true knowledge of the universe.

It is only in seeking the truth that there can be a world of reciprocal trust. Its opposite produces evil and hatred.

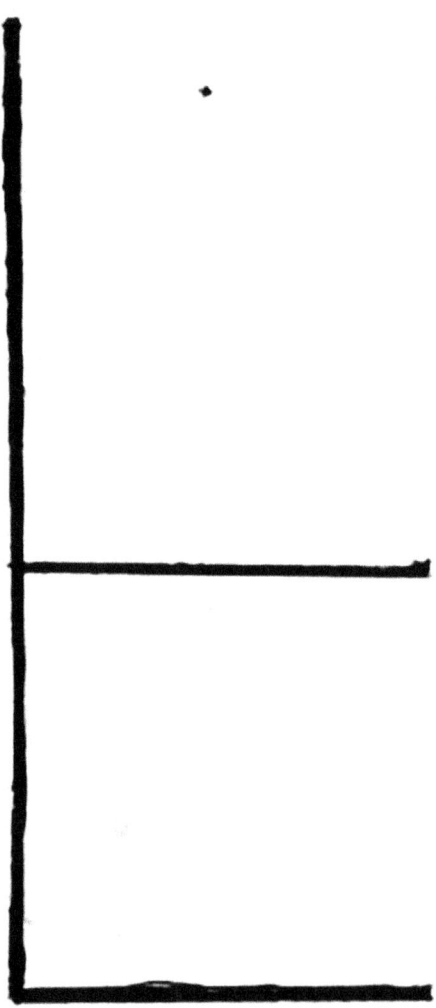

YANFINDI: is the sign of destiny. According to the sign men have different fates, some will have happiness, others in difficulty. It also indicates the existence of two things, that is, couples: earth and heaven, man and woman, good and evil.

KOFINDI is the opposite of the preceding sign, so no being can escape destiny. The acceptance of destiny is a belief in the master of the universe. It treats psychologically human thought to have faith in destiny and not to undertake anything contrary to others.

KISSANGO : indicates the 4 paths. The path of the master (sema), the path of the supervisor (Koté), the path of the operator (yangoyoli), and the path of the initiates (Gayé). These 4 paths suggests that each path has a different role to play in relations to each others.

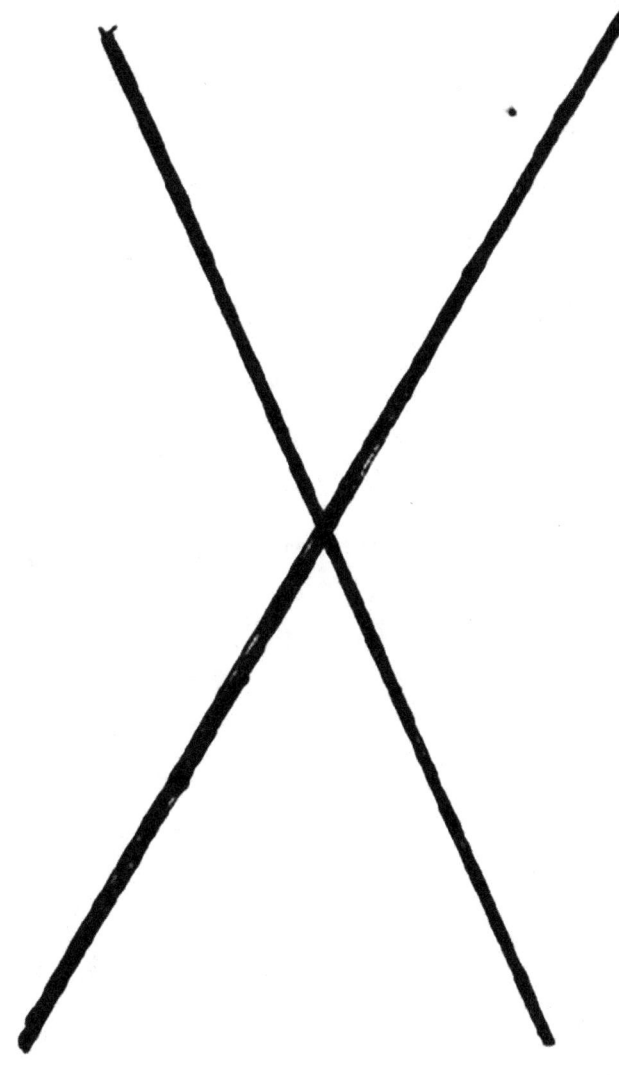

TOUNKHOUMA : This hieroglyphic sign indicates that the four quarters of the world poles: east, west, south, and north. According to the diagram, days as they occur has 4 cardinal points and indicates there is movement between the earth's axis, which prevents the meeting of any two poles. According to the days, there is a permanent movement of the earth.

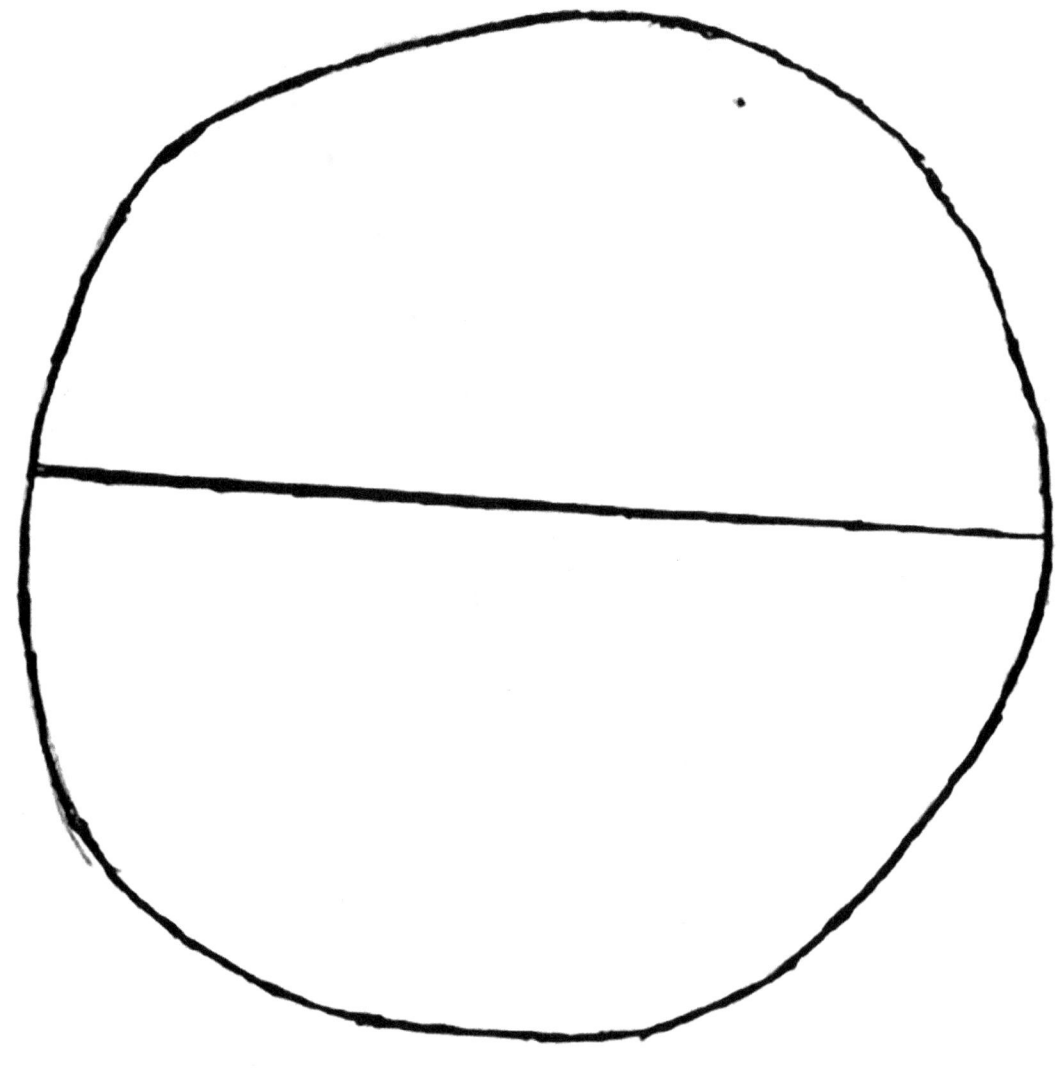

KIRASO: means that once the initiates arrives within the school setting, knowledge will be discovered and will lead the initiates to know the twelve signs and their meanings. Kiraso reminds us that knowledge extends to several domains, astronomy, botany, counters and legends etc ... are areas of laga.

Sekan: by definition, Sekan is the acquisition of knowledge. This sign represents "Sema" or master. Sema is the person who attains knowledge after the stage of initiation. His duty and right is to serve the community.

Chapter IV: An Explanation of Select Articles of the Charter of KEMEKIYAH

In its first definition, the definition represents knowledge. In second definition, binyè (respect) or knowledge is defined as having great importance. Below, the following are subsets of the symbol below:

Doing good with respect
Sacrificing is a respect
Sacrificing is a hope
Money relieves man's life

The burden of the family belongs to man and by giving his right hand.
The first step is the man must do the following:
Get up very early
Take courage
Fight against poverty

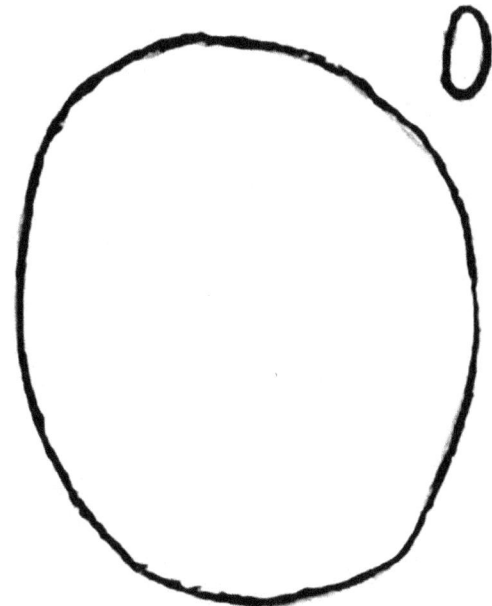

Nothing goes beyond union
Creating village groups (kile)
Only one must kill the supplied but does not take
Make your bodies and places of gathering clean

One never confides his behavior to another
The union enlarges the mind of man
A public man lives with the people
When playing musical instruments, it is to attract the world
To become important it is necessary to choose the men
Union is a sacred act.

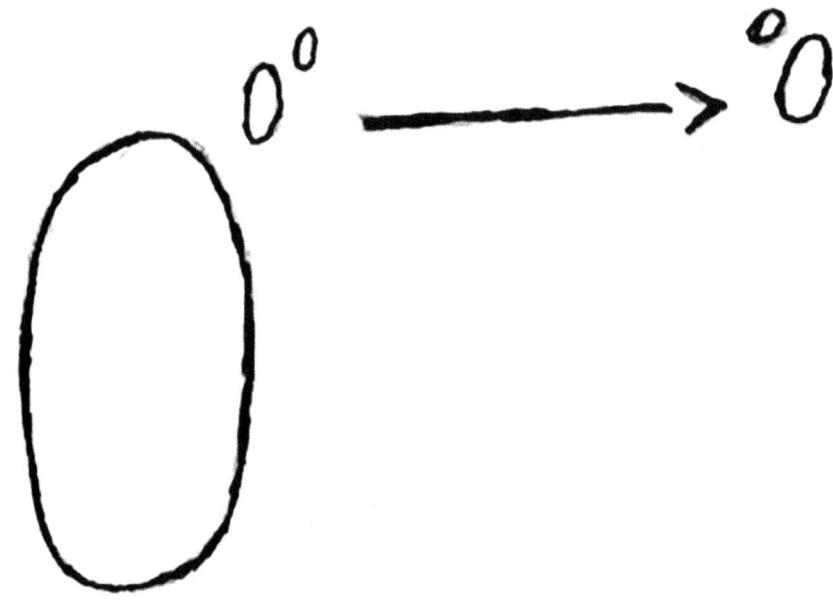

Never take part in a war that you do not know the beginning
If your bowl serving is small, take patience, one day it will be great.
Whatever the forest, the bird will find its nest
Cover containers that contains the food
A drop of water is a life.

Never interrupt a speech in the middle
There is no fact without cause
Learn curiosity with questions asked
Patience is a path for the hunter
Yams are harvested because of its fruit
Protect your reputation and the legacy of your family's name

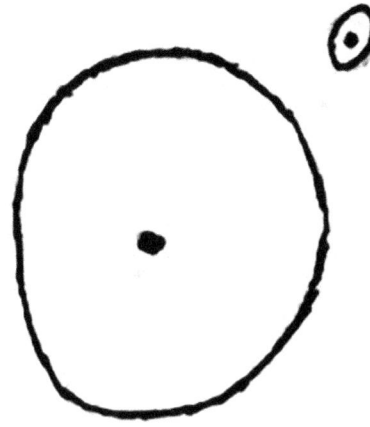

To make war within yourself is self-consciousness.
Finding friends is to find hope
The law has no shame
Say what's next, it does not diminish anything in you
Three beads seek a single fact

The wicked never has peace in his/her heart
The good always benefits
Know that if the black ant stings you, the red ant will make save the lives of your loved ones
A healthy tooth is not removed
Never try to imitate someone you are not

Power is not the prerogative of anyone
The world is very old
Learn the law
The lie does not rule over the truth
Defend the community
Search continuously for the path of truth

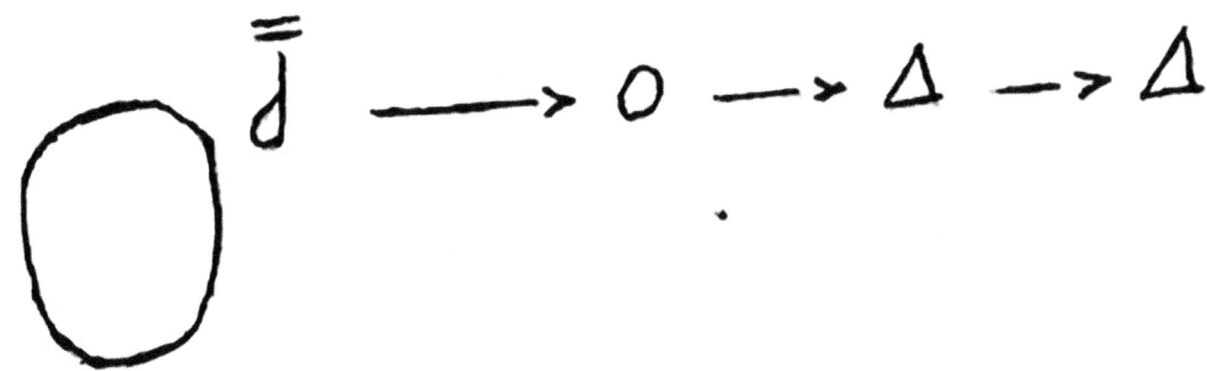

A leader is born, one does not become one
The quality of clothing depends ones the means
We start saddle wearing on the right
A little skewer little enough
Food is good for the chef
The people must be at ease with the national heritage

Unity is strength
Know your morals and traditions
Men of the same clan name are the same
Men with the same surname must love each other
One man must sacrifice himself to redeem his community
The relative is a consumable leak

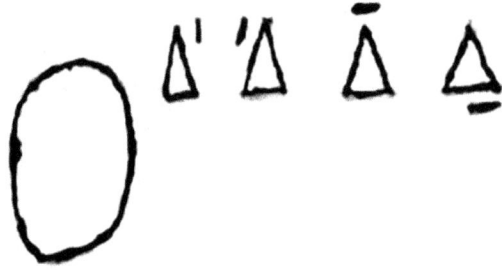

Find wide areas
Scatter in space
The departure of from the truth seems small, but its end is grand
Large communities always have the good
Let the good marriage be celebrated between us
Give the name of your first sons to your fathers and mothers

Do not kill
The one who kills, will not be seen after the dead
Hope is for the one who hopes
Crime is a source of unity
The soul must be protected

Share knowledge
The one who kills is cursed
Create reclamation places
Do not hurt yourself
Protect yourself in safety
Be humble
An enlightened mind is a clean soul

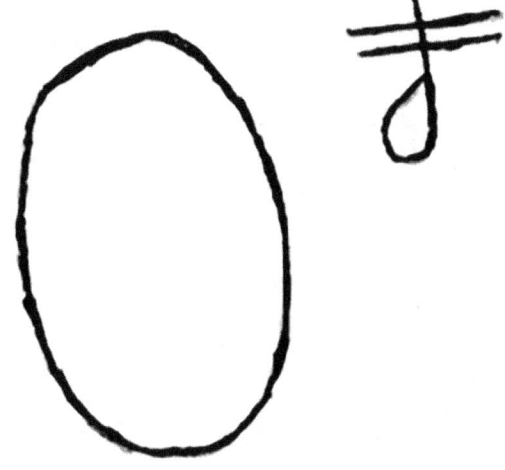

Be militant for your homeland
Be an isolationist when needed
The security of the country is a law
Be honest about your country
Plant fruit trees
Sacrifice yourself for your community

Translate your dreams into reality
Be aware of who is betraying
Show the right way to your children
Build your nations in happiness
Choose the right habitat locations

Develop the territory

Let us love each other
Do not create enemies amongst yourselves
Apologize at the appropriate time
Live with joy
Accept all forms of voluntary contribution
Bring help to those in need

Make the neighborhood a kinship
Speak the truth while you are joking
Marry
your family
Exchange agricultural areas
Make invitations
Make good neighbors

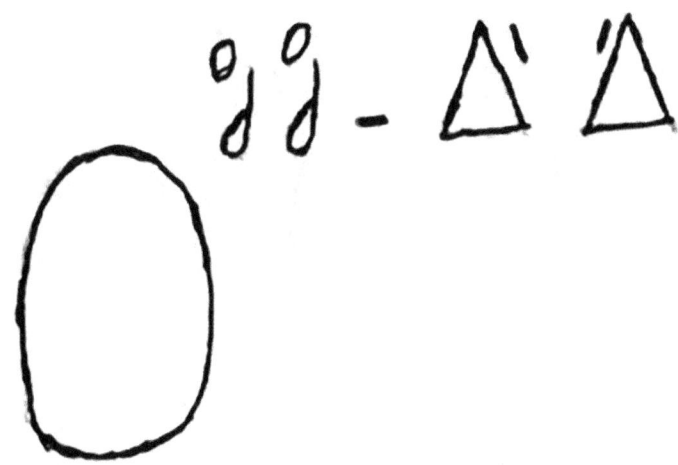

Lying never takes form and does not survive
Do not give your energy to lies
lies smells bad
The lie does not grow
The lie does not have long life
Combat a lie with honesty

Be honest
Have a moral integrity
Lying does not give the personality
Avoid lying
Find the path of truth

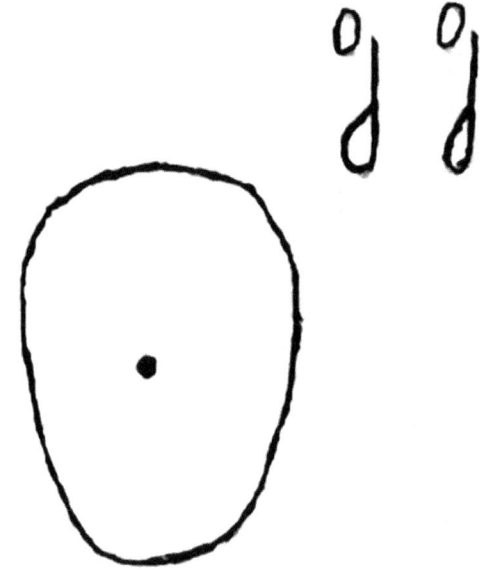

SOCIAL AND TERRITORIAL ORGANIZATION

SILIKI: Brilliant personalities are seen for their material goods, their knowledge, or the public power
This person is fair
He/She builds the country
He/She is a man of knowledge
He/She shares knowledge
He/She develops education

He/She is an example of someone who is of good conduct or models justice
He/She illuminates doubt
He brings people together
He/She is rich man
He/She has a good position
He/She helps to chase famine

Lasiri; Slave owner or large landowner
Purveyor of hope
Having a great family connection
A great public man
Male or female person

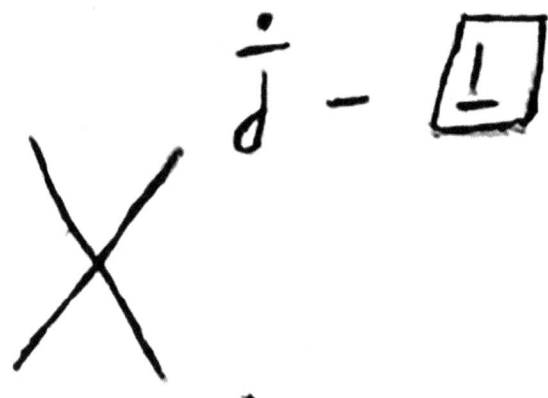

Having an average
Full authority
Having several houses
Possess good visions
Have self-control

Provide projects of vision

KHÖRE: belongs to nobody and nobody belongs to it
It is self-sufficient
It is not in charge of anyone
It is not in need
It is initiated
It is humble

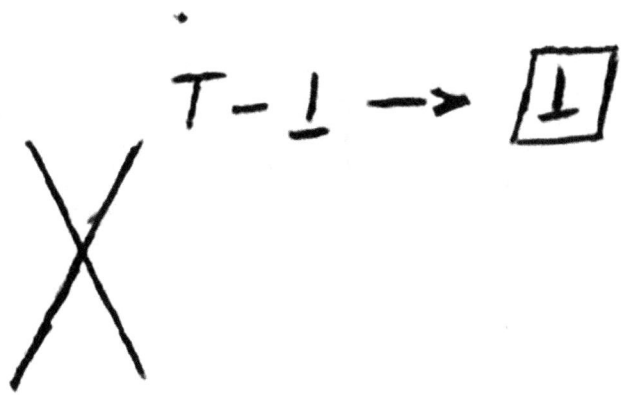

It speaks well, quiet, and discreet
It lives in the union
It arranges

It is enough

KONYI: is a slave who under held against his/her will, dominated or subjected to captivity
Captive of war or purchased
Sold
Caught
A former prisoner of war
An ex-communicate by misdemeanor

He/She is not ashamed
He/She does not represent himself/herself
He/She does not control his actions
He/She can be resold

A slave woman or man can be married

The EMPIRE: a vast territory comprising kingdoms (Bokhigbe)
Large territory
Has several states
Based on a single constitution
Comprises of a unified army
Good political organization

Good solidarity
High power
A rich population
A strong army

Strong adherence to patriotism

The country or kingdom is under an empire
Kandet is the supreme king
Must be a country of abundance
Country of high vegetation
Country of high vegetation
Land of the nobles
A country of mining resources

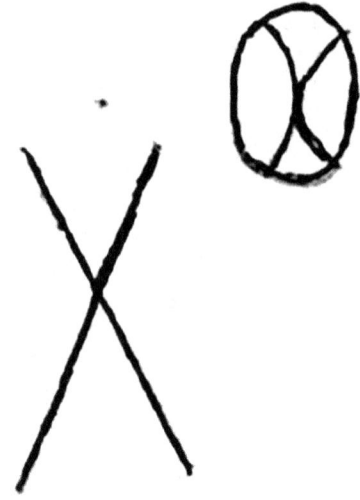

A country of hope
Country of marshes
Country with the known universe
Country of assistance
Country of teachers

Country of currency

Mangueta: is the capital of the state.
Kitidé: is the court of justice i.e. meeting place
Place of discretion
a Unit or a place of decision

The order
Place of regrouping of men
Location of justice
An economic power
A place of distribution

place of happiness

Ta: is the city
Ya: is the place

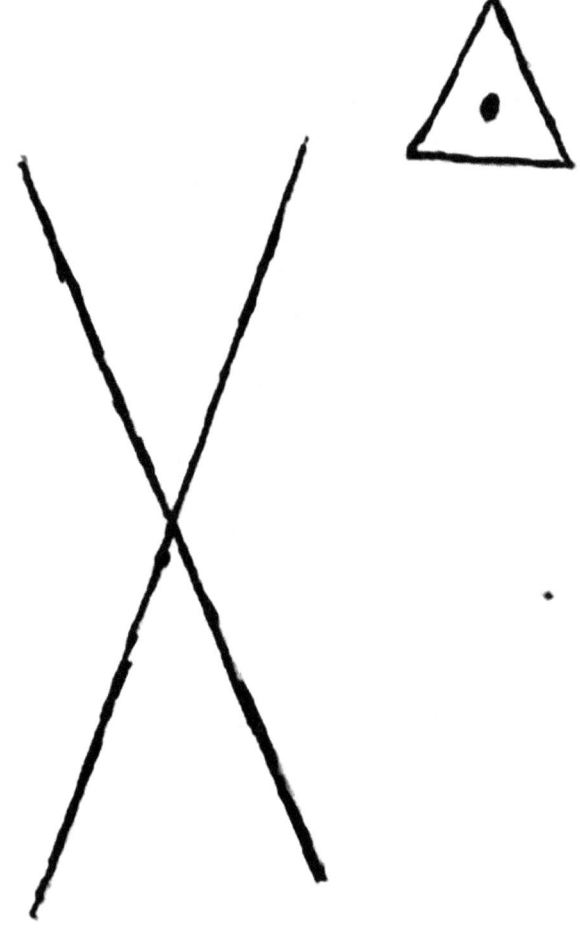

Ka: is the earth

Dakha: the hamlet
Dondeé the small hamlet
Foundations of plantations
Place of food
Proliferate food
Security Location

A place of fruits
Develop crop fields
Central location of all economic data
A place of help
Storage place or location

Chapter V: The Meaning of the FEDAKHIE or FEDALI

SERVICE OF FENDALIS

- Good knowledge

- Bad knowledge

- Bad, killed, gutter, etc.

- Evil between two people

- The world

- The leader, a respected

- The family or a house

= Relation

The tomb

= Good work

= Help

= A patient

= Good

= One language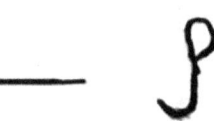

= Exchange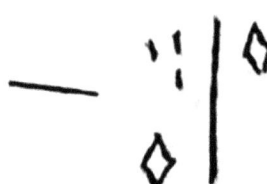

= The bowl

= The matrimonial home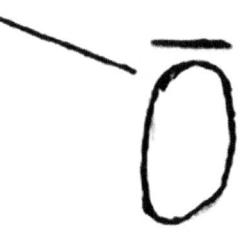

= The fruit

Three days

The Military

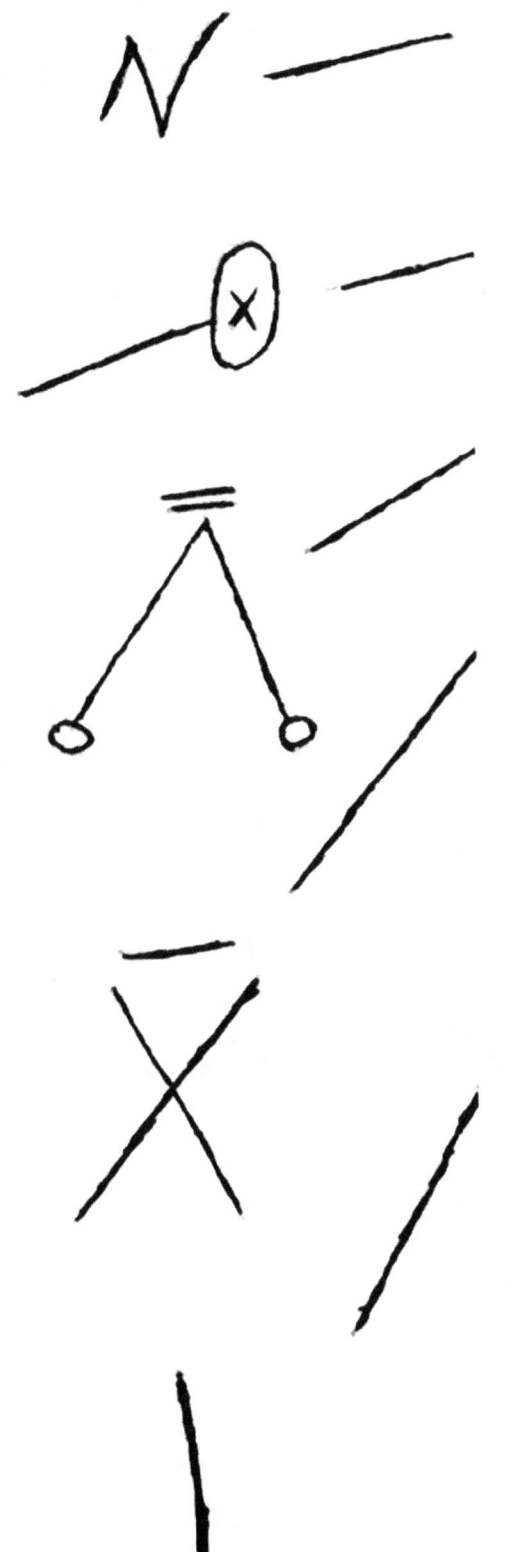

= The mountain

= The game

The Government

= Good judgment

= The supervisor

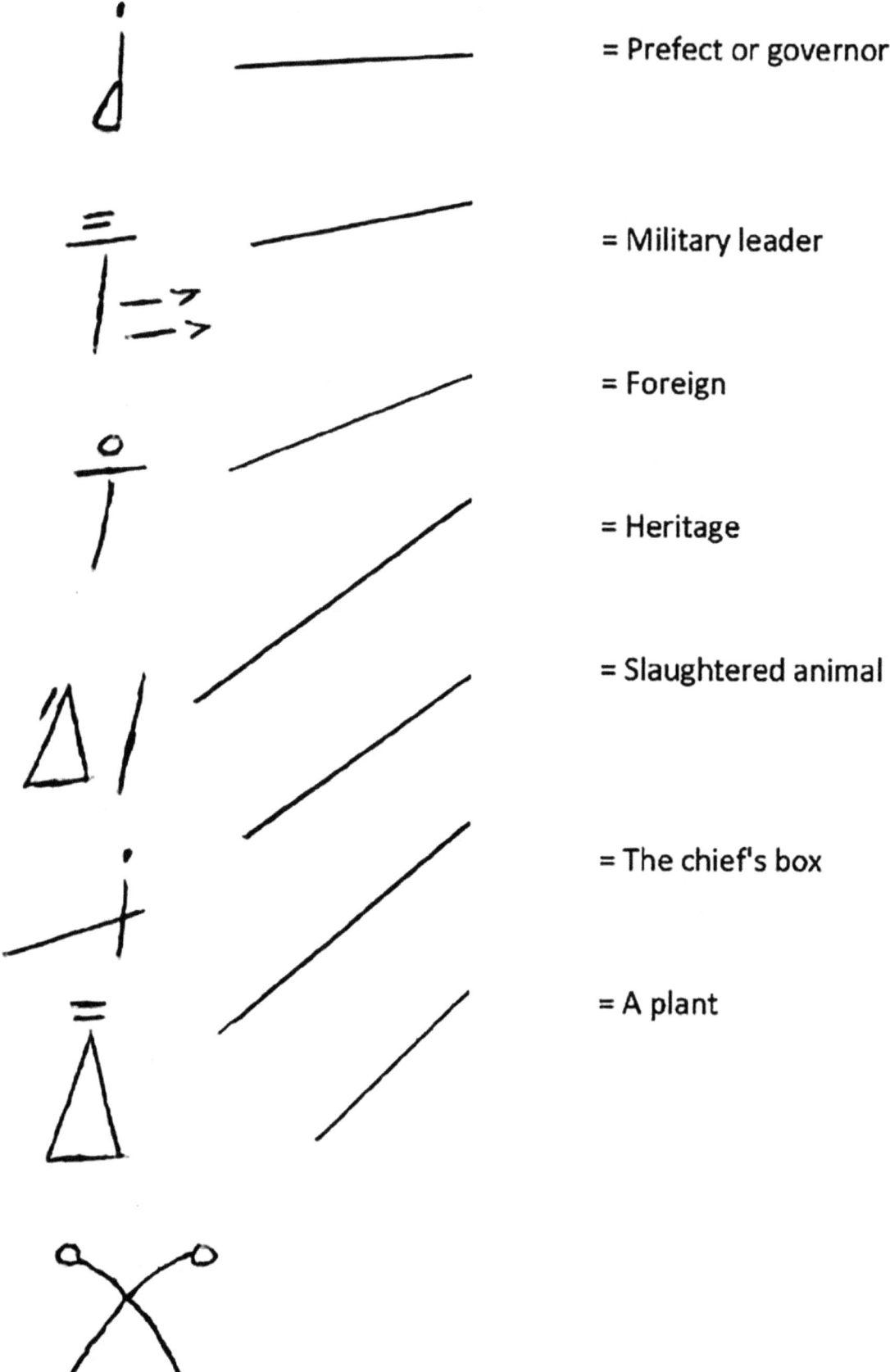

SERVICE OF FENDALIS (Continued6)

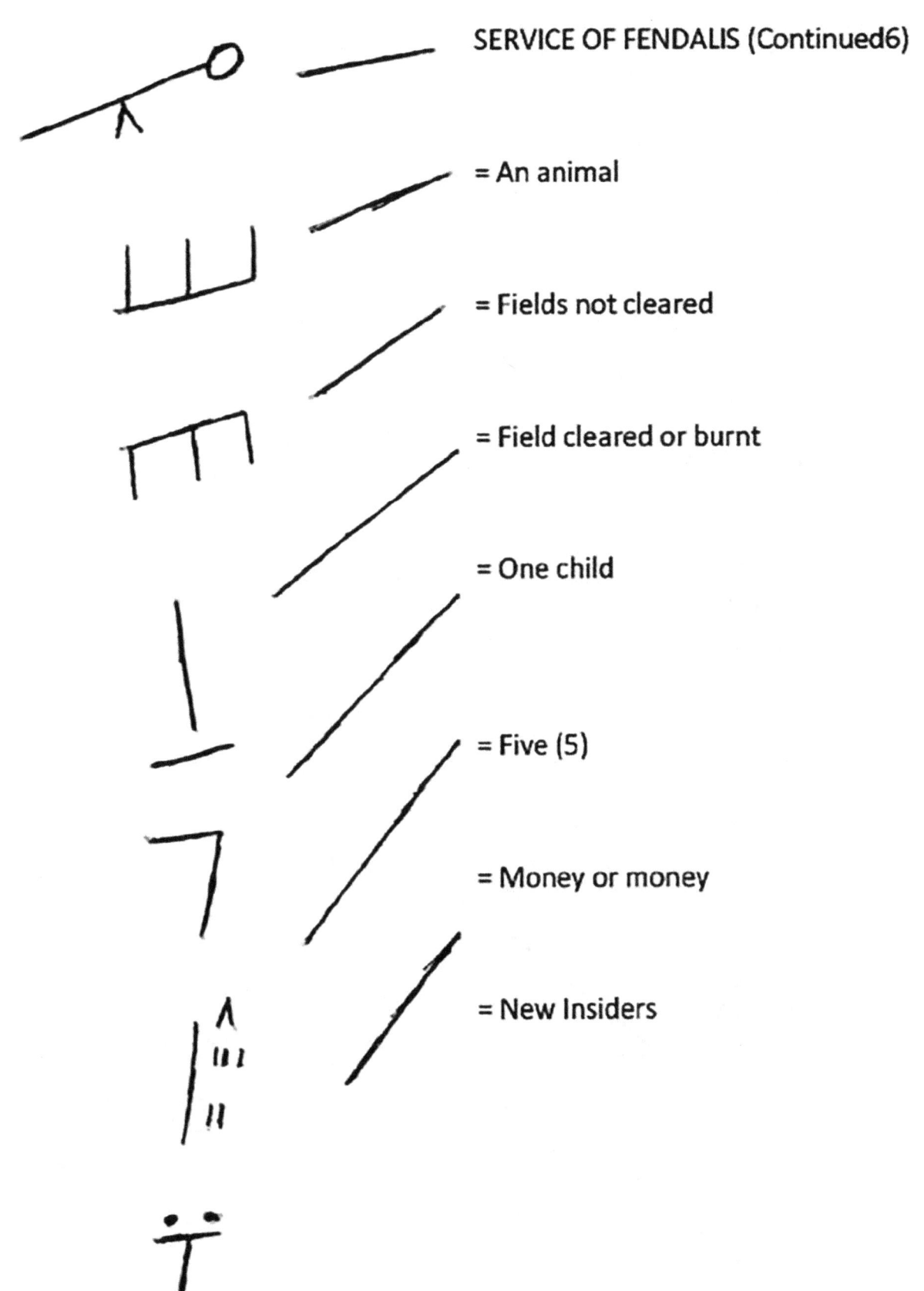

= An animal

= Fields not cleared

= Field cleared or burnt

= One child

= Five (5)

= Money or money

= New Insiders

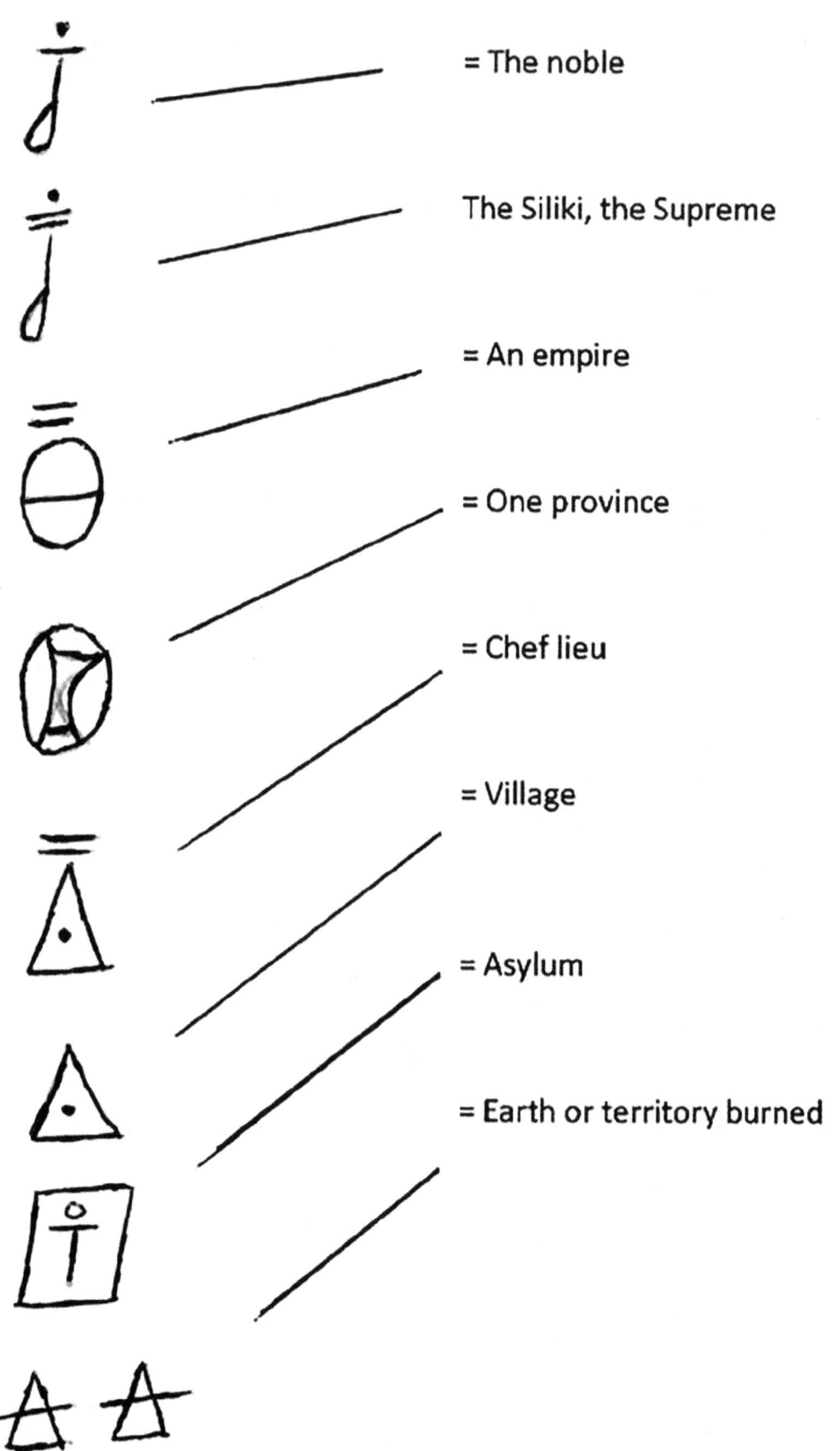

CHAPITRE VI : An Interpretation of Select Articles of KEMEKIRIYAH

AN INTERPRETATION OF SELECT KEMEKIRIYA ARTICLES

Article 1: Go for useful knowledge

This law was taught in laga and began in the first days of the initiation. Knowledge acquisition is the inner motivation of a human being. This information once acquired assist the individual for the advancement of training and development of his/her community. In the social sense, it values the person in knowing how to choose the company of good friends, or companionship. It also gives strength for the betterment or empowerment of one's actions toward, parents or fellow citizens, and a serves as a means of grasping better opportunities for success. To be endowed with the powers of good, in this case, knowledge, affords one to succeed in any field, trade or objective. The quality above is a necessity for all men to seek what is good and in abandoning the influences of evil.

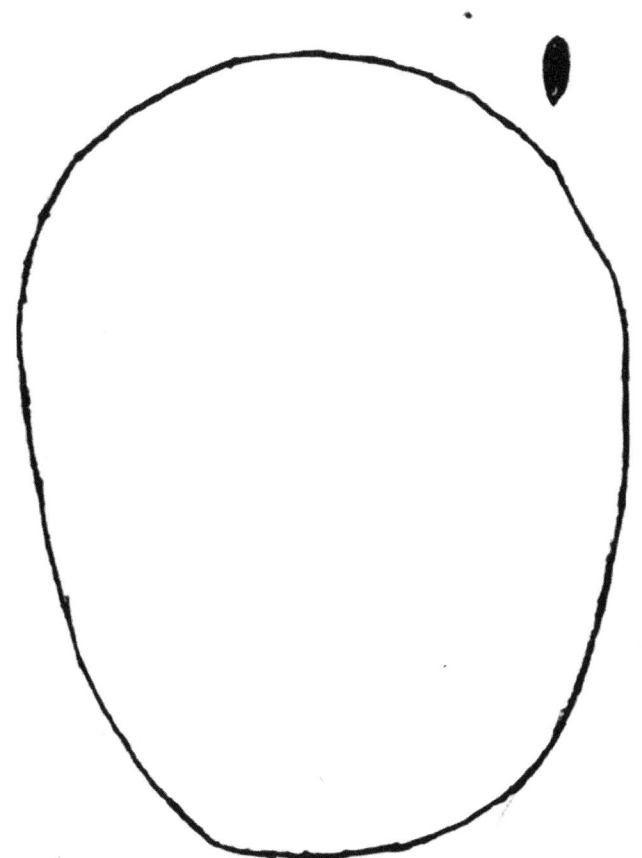

Article 2: Unite

This second law calls for unity. In human organizations, all facts or actions are summarized in a harmonious faction i.e. a group, family, clan, tribe, or people in which the individuals value its productive forces. They must work together to establish the standards they desire. In addition, unity is not only moral but also material because it demonstrates adequate measures, in which all is possible only when productive forces are collectively combined to produce a bulk of production. The Sosos invented several forms of unity which are: kilés, lanyi, lankhoundé, Kaya, etc.

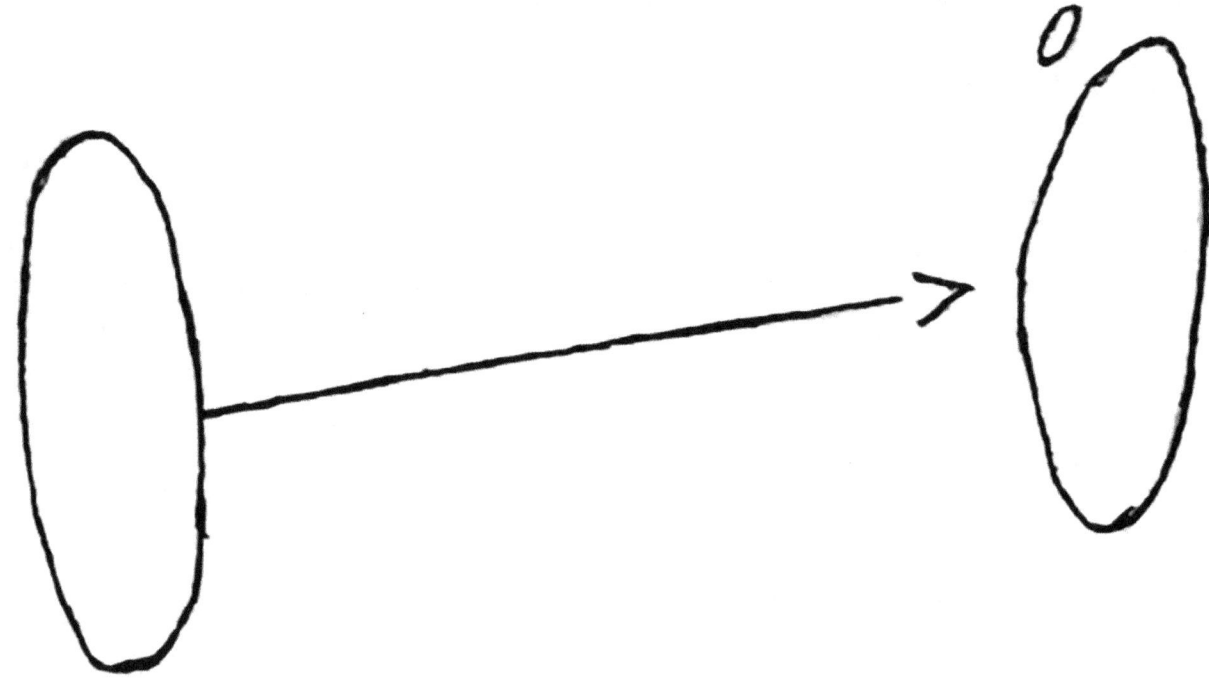

Article 5: The exercise of power is transparent, it is within the reach of each family.

This article seeks to dismantle the alternation of power in the Soso. Power is not the prerogative of a family or a clan, but rather the choice of the people and for individual members of the community who may feel interested in exercising their powers. Depending on the certain events, leaders emerged from various parts of the community and may explain why the kings or emperors of Soso came from different clans, as power was transitory.

For example: Soso Dantouma etati un Bangoura; Manguè Frigui was a Camara; Mangue Bouye was a Sylla; Soso Soumaoro was a soumah. These striking examples serve as witnesses to that of the Sosso's empire and have always been the source of democracy by using alternating power between the different clans.

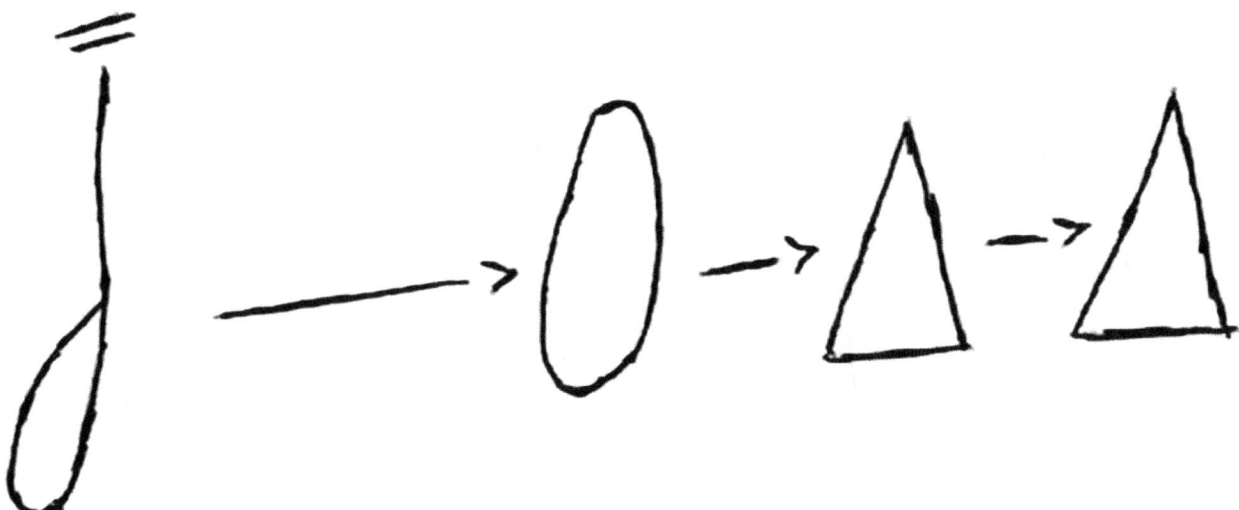

Article 6: Of consensus, villages are inhabited by patronyms

In Soso villages, when a stranger crosses the threshold of the community and presents himself before a family, he is welcomed by fresh water. After respectful greetings, the head of the family offers him a warm welcome, then asks him/her about his surname; if he/she answers "Camara," and shows him/her immediately where the Camara clan origin is, he/she joins the ancestral clan of his/her heritage. These instructions are traditionally respected in the Soso culture.

Article 7: Do not Kill

Killing is an act or crime forbidden by the Djallon Soso. This was a long established way of life before the arrival of the Arabs and Westerners. This immoral act was severely repressed and condemned. Djallon Soso considers that killing of one's neighbor is a force of conflict between family, but also between the clans and could end with a declaration of war. Moreover, he further considers that prohibition is a source of peace between the members of the same community and that it cultivates the image of peace and love, and provide those involved in tensions with their neighbors to seek love and forgiveness.

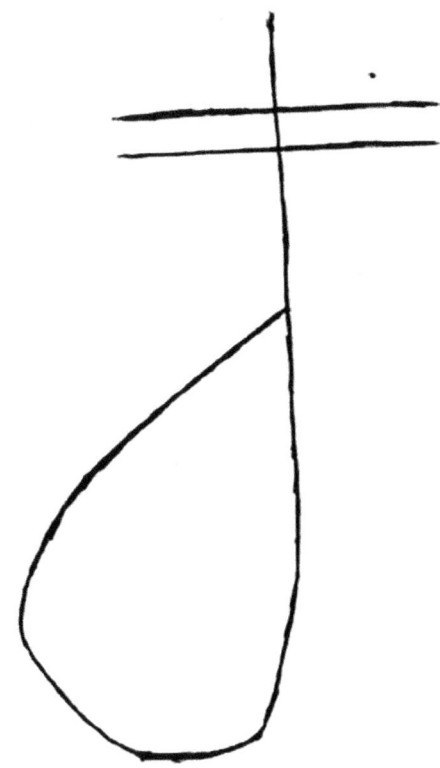

Article 9: Be serious in the truth and in the kinship relationship

The sanakhouya is a djalonka word, means to be added to each other. It was adopted for the first time in Kirina under the palable tree called Kiri or the baobab. In 1077, during the global reform for the Djalon Soso. The law recognized and authorized members of different clans who have marital ties to establish unions. The rule applies to life, as living is part of marriage. Marriage signifies the union or alliance between sons, brothers, and sisters. Those who married their cousins considers the marriage as a joke. Example Camara and les Sylla; The Bangoura and the Soumah.

Article 10: Do not lie because lying never has a long life

The lie is in Article 10. A person who lies is seen as the person who promotes hatred. Once a lie is told, the Soso culture reminds you, by saying «iwoulé 10». This signifies that when you lie, you lie to article 10 of the Kemekiriya charter. The Sosos considers that this lie is at the source of many evils and can also trigger hatreds. When the initiates are trained in the image of truth, they are seen as human capital for the community. Men from laga are seen as examples in the community for their honesty.

Article 15: Do not commit adultery

Adultery is the most repressed act in the Soso culture. Every initiated person do not address adultery, young girls and boys are subjected to a responsible education, which does not allow them to commit such an act.

A Soso girl could be solicited as a friend by a youngster otherwise become her lover called «kelé». The colas nuts are presented by the boy's buddies to the girl's family while waiting for the parents to unanimously give their blessings to the young girl or young boy until to marriage. Once this girl is accompanied to her husband's house, and she finds herself a virgin, a meal of honor is offered by the in-laws to the husband of the woman. Once the young person takes the kelé, and accepts the girl, together, the couple celebrates this honor. This practice remains a traditional practice in today's villages.

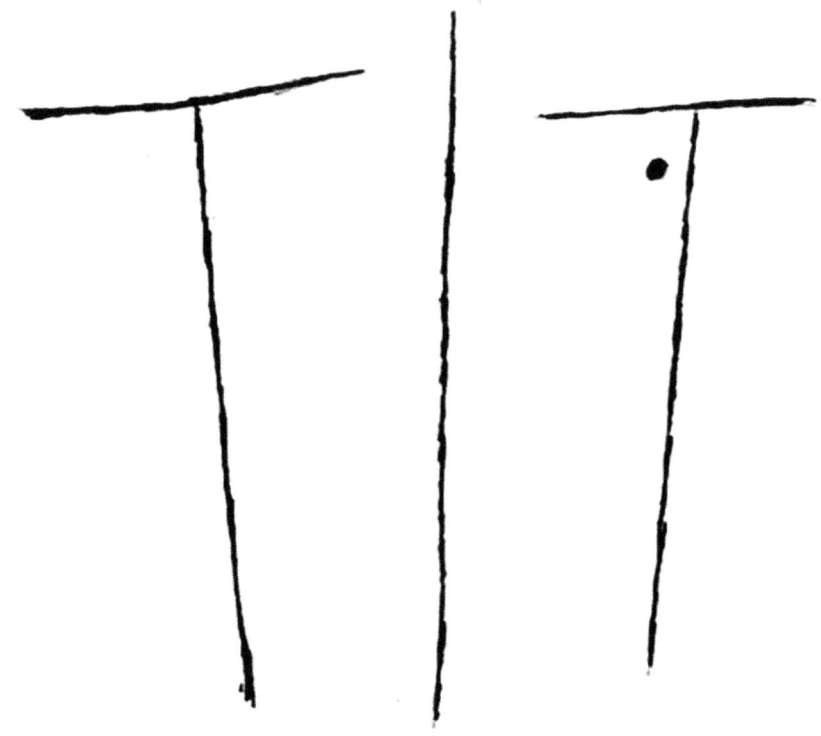

Article 23: Treat the sick even if they are needy

In Soso communities, it is recommended to come to the rescue of the sick, without asking for anything. Women and men who are healers used their knowledge to serve the community. As customary, the sick only had to present the evils from which they were suffering, and the healer's duty is to bring all possible treatment. If he could not heal the sick, another "guerrisseur" [or healer] take over until he/she recovers from his/her illness. Strong men/women were often the chosen ones selected to carry out the task of healing since they were able to move from one village to another in search of the sick, and able to offer free services. After the patient is cured, members of the ill, if they had the opportunity could offer presents to the healer according to their wealth. This act was a sign of respect and gratitude.

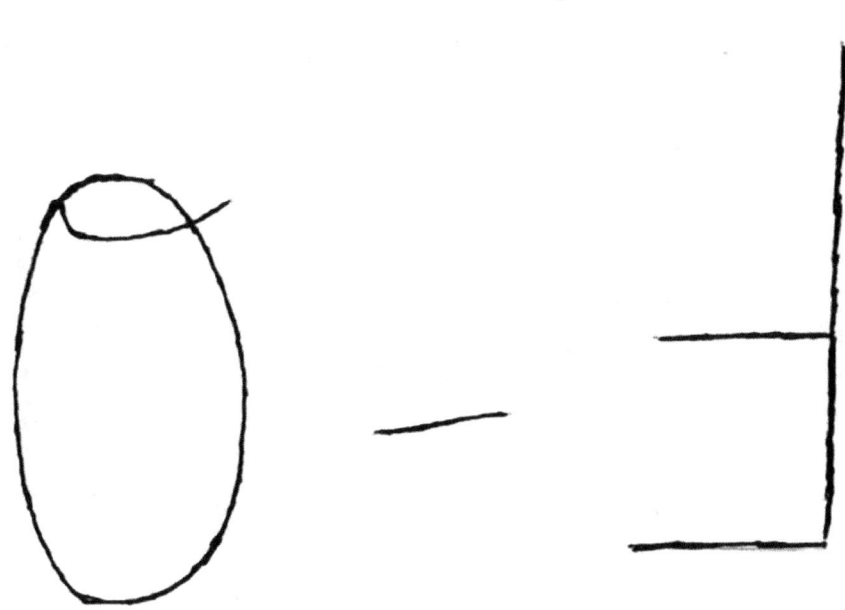

Article 31: Do not pick fruits before maturity

In Soso culture, the planting of fruits were under the control of the community led by the Kountigui. He is the oldest of the clan. They consider that the fruits can not be harvested without the permission of the Kountigui. His leadership ascertained the prevention of waste by children. To preserve this ordinance, fruits were not harvested before they are fully edible. A sanction was issued by the court of justice «Birinkha», if an act of disobedience was committed by a member, the right to eat the fruit was withdrawn. Fruit production was removed from that family's privilege and divided into three parts: first for the village, second for the notables, and the final section was given to the Kountigui. This law was respected by all members of the community, only when the Koutigui orders the harvest could crops be eaten. This act was called, «Tonyi».

Article 41: Kandet the leader and his entourage are only one

This article discusses the existence of the government and their organization. It demands that any established agreement or consensus, of acts and decisions, must be taken up by the governmental team called, «Manguè Sanyi». Any selected or elected leader of the people usually takes office on the 41st day. During the first 40 days, and at the withdrawal denomé «Madoukoui.». Every morning the balafonists instrument is used to awake the king and offered, "Mangue, known as a melody of rejoicing. The Kountiguis provides him with the necessary advice for the proper conduct of the affairs of the community. He is then required to learn the 100 articles of Kemekiriya and its applications in times of peace and war. On the day of his swearing in ceremony, all that he needs will be handed to him on the day of the investiture, immediately by the former chief and before he takes an oath.

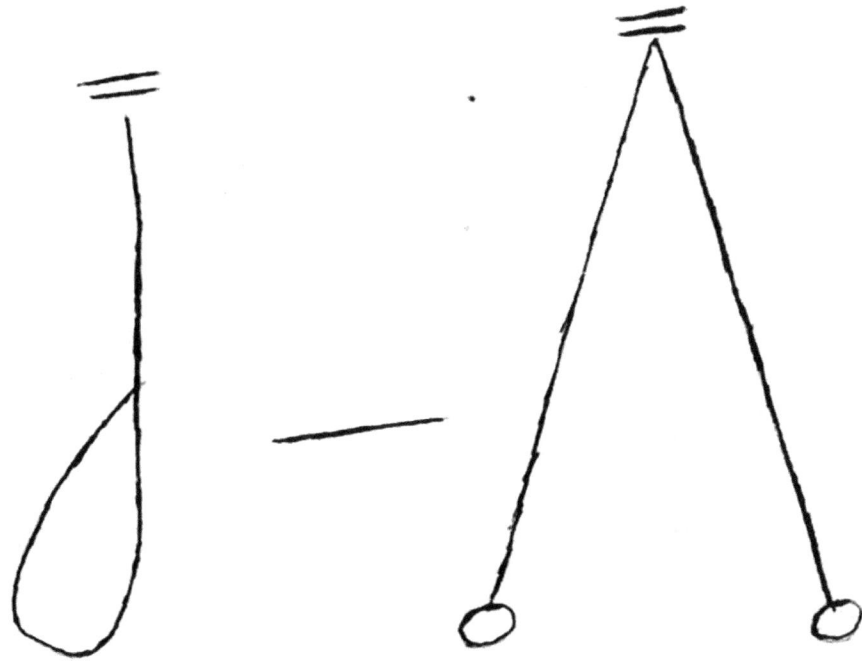

Soso Antiquity Culture And Civilization

DO YOURSELF YOUR PREDICTIONS

Fendali Founoun Firin is the oldest of the alphabets. The Sema (Master) in charge of initiation in Soso culture and their people who invented it. Each letter of fendali has a hidden meaning and can, when drawn, predict the future.

Gan:
The oracle insists on the importance of the message of the second drawing.

Dera:
Is the sign of the beginning, a slogan to achieve your ends: discretion! As the beginning remain silent and wait for your hour, for the enemy does not turn into a friend, nor lies actually tells Soso wisdom.

Yafindi:
⌐ A complicity between man and woman, if you are a woman you will find support with a man, if you are a man, a woman appreciates your ambitions.

Kofindi:
⌐ Beware, there is a high risk of conflicts with serious consequences. Avoid provocations.

Kisango:
∉ Anyone who does not know his story knows nothing at all: "if you do not know where you are going then go back where you come from".

Kikeren:
| An important news story. This can of course be a letter, but also an information for you capital.

Khounsa:
ϒ
The oracle warns you against a risk of illusion, show yourself cautious, pay attention to false hopes.

Tounkhouma:
Θ Announces satisfaction, success. If you are at the bottom of the wells, the end of the troubles is looming. Satisfaction is often signed with a return of money

Sansogué: Kiraso:

⊣ Thunderbolt, predestined encounter, blessed days, fusion. In this encounter, a perfect supernatural agreement.

Φ No one grants hope if it starts well, it will end badly.

Sanfindi: Sekan:

⊢ With a close, quarrels arise from nothing and multiply at work. Be careful to escape the wrong move.

You will be able to dance on the summit of the mountains, without fear of falling .... This is the best of oracles. God protects you happiness is at your door.

⊢ With a close, quarrels arise from nothing and multiply at work. Be careful to escape the wrong move.

You will be able to dance on the summit of the mountains, without fear of falling .... This is the best of oracles. God protects you happiness is at your door.

To play, put these fandali on a ball-shaped paper and pull one, and then you will return to the corresponding explanation.

EXPLANATION

These words enabled us to know and fix the names of the Emperors, and subsequently the duration of their reigns.

This allowed the Djalonsossos to count example: 32 Sansogue Khounsa; Khounse dera; 26 Khounsa Kofindi; 23 Khounsa Sansogue; 29 Khounsa Kirasso; 28 Khounsa Tounkhouma.

Which means that the Sosos knew how to count; Kikeren, 1 Khounsa 2, Sansogue 3, Sanfindi 4, Yafindi 5, Kofindi 6, Kinsango 7, Tounkhouma 8, Kirasso 9.

The duration of the Soso empire is 158 years, the sum of the times of reign of the 6 Emperors of Soso. When the time of reign of the Emperors Soso 158 is added to the end of the empire of Ghana 1077, it is well, the end of the reign of the last king of Soso 1235, that of Kandet Soumaro.

CONCLUSION

Without wasting time, the young researchers should start documenting the history of African antiquity. There is a quote which states, "Africa is the cradle of humanity. " As African, we invite you to document all ancient cultural facts of Africa's civilization. Our intent is not to downplay cultural and scientific accomplishments of our culture, but to commit ourselves to the enhancing our traditional African values. This document records our history of the origin of man, as the history of LAGA dates back to the age of Antiquity.

Meaning of certain word

1. Kandet: Emperor
2. Santiguigbe: Viceroy
3. Santigui: Minister
4. Khali: Governor
5. Kountigui: Member of Parliament
6. Kayana: Assembly
7. Laga: School
8. Kouye: The Universe
9. Marigui: God
10. Batui: Prayer
11. Tounkhouma: The World
12. Khanta: Life
13. Lakhata: Beyond
14. Ka: The Earth
15. Ya: The place
16. Lasiri: The noble
17. Siliki: Great renown
18. Bari: The ancestors
19. Koly: General of the Army

BIBLIOGRAPHY

The Semas (the instructors of the Sossoka tradition)

1- Fire Elhadj Memodou Bangoura (Coyah)
2- Fire Sira Sekhou Camara (Coyah)
3- Fire Elhadj Malik Conte (Boffa)
4- Fode Ali Gassama (Forecariah)
5- Fire Commander Amirou Camara (Sougueta - Kindia)
6- Professor Salif Sylla (Conakry)
7- Hadja Mbambe Soumah (Coyah)
8- Koly Bangoura (Bentouraya)
9- Kandet Bouhari Camara (Conakry)

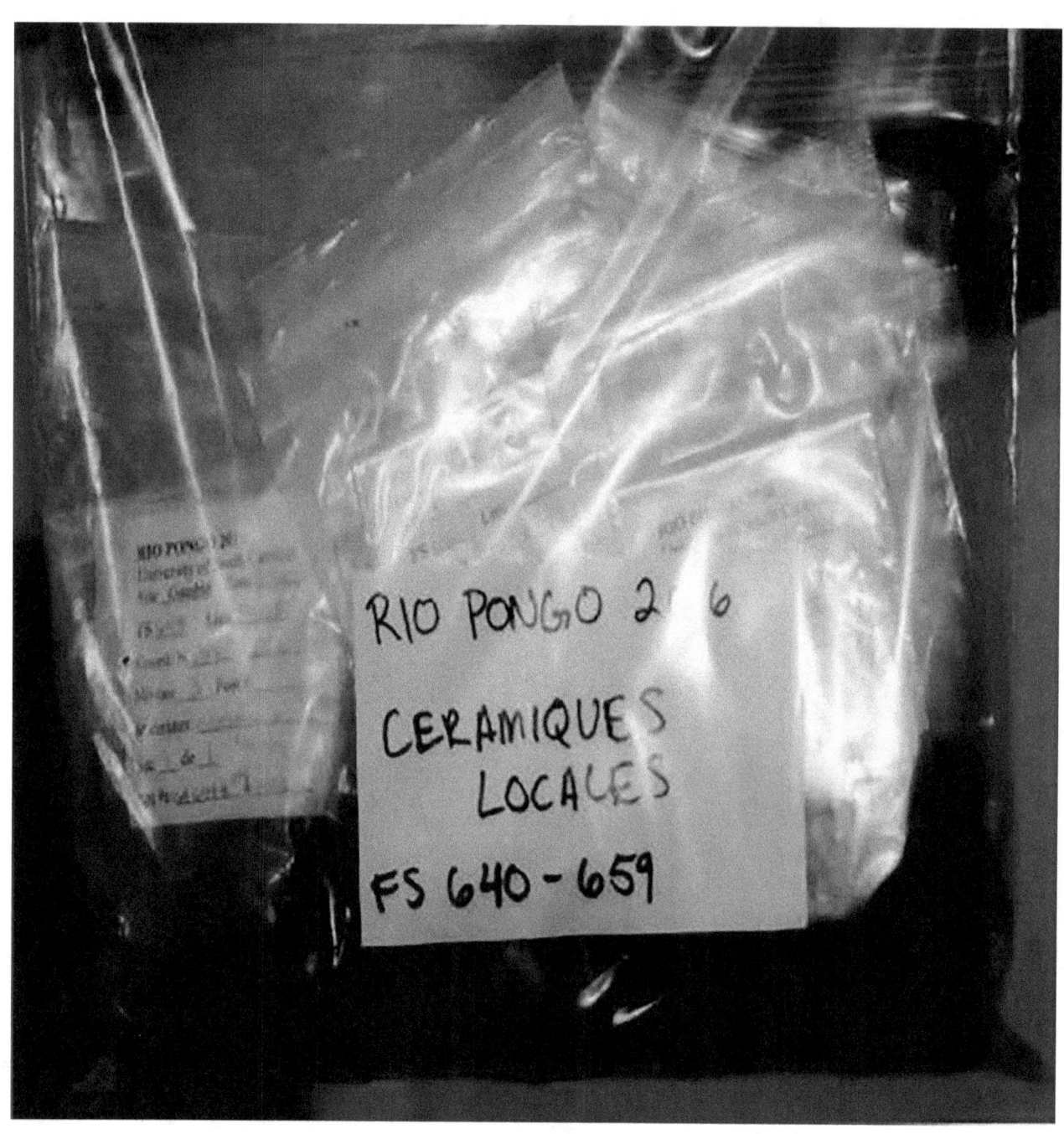

Search Guinean American Archeology

CBG: Environmental Study (Laboratory National Museum of Guinea)

Museum of Guinea

ABOUT THE AUTHOR

Mohamed Bentoura Bangoura alias Mohamed Ben Bangoura is born on August 1st 1964 in Coyah-city in the Soumbouya. Cayah is a city of the Guinea situated at 50 Km of Conakry, the Capital. He is descended from the marabout Karamokho Bentoura, his great grandfather and great erudite Marabou Fode Aly Bangoura, his great father. He did his Koranic and religious studies until 1981. His studied at the French school led him to the Baccalaureate in 1993, and completed his higher education studies, where he received a diploma of superior studies option sociology in 1988.

Since 1990, he has worked as a state official, first as a teacher, then as prefect in several localities of the country, and currently serving in the Ministry of Territorial Administration and Decentralization. His curiosity has led him to conduct research in many areas for more than 30 years. These research have enabled him to discover the Kore Sebeli alphabet, the etymology of the Soso language, Bentoura figures, Kemekiriya charter and other upcoming publications.

www.ingramcontent.com/pod-product-compliance
Lightning Source LLC
LaVergne TN
LVHW081544060526
838200LV00048B/2201